THE MINISTER AS FAMILY COUNSELOR

THE MINISTER AS FAMILY COUNSELOR

Charles William Stewart

ABINGDON
NASHVILLE

THE MINISTER AS FAMILY COUNSELOR

Library of Congress Cataloging in Publication Data

STEWART, CHARLES WILLIAM.
The minister as family counselor.
Bibliography: p.
1. Pastoral counseling.   2. Family psychotherapy.
3. Family—Religious life.   I.   Title.
BV4012.2.S73   253.5   79-10854

ISBN 0-687-26955-5

Scripture quotations noted RSV are from the Revised Standard Version
Common Bible, copyrighted © 1973 by the Division of Christian
Education of the National Council of Churches of Christ in the U.S.A.

Scripture quotations noted NEB are from the New English Bible,
copyright © the Delegates of the Oxford University Press and the Syndics
of the Cambridge University Press, 1961, 1970.

MANUFACTURED BY THE PARTHENON PRESS AT
NASHVILLE, TENNESSEE, UNITED STATES OF AMERICA

*To the students of marriage and the family
from whom I have learned
and whom I have taught and supervised*

Contents

Preface

Before setting out to write this book I attended a day-long seminar on psychoanalytic therapy followed by a three-day workshop on "relationship enhancement." In the first, Freudian theory and practice were set forth as the treatment of choice for psychoneurotics; in the second, a learning model was developed as an approach to solving family problems. I became aware again of the fact that schools with different theoretical models of personality and norms for the healthy family vie for the attention of the public.

Fortunately, in the period between these two conferences, my wife, Alma, and I spent a morning with Howard and Charlotte Clinebell, friends over the years, simply talking and being ourselves. We spoke of what we had experienced since we last met; in particular, our lives with our families, the pain, brokenness, separation and death of family members, as well as the growth, joy, and happiness in friendships, the love bonds and support of families and communities. The presence of our two daughters at the table with us added spice to the conversation.

In reflecting on the week's experience, Alma and I concluded that theories, in particular overgeneralized ones, are secondary to relationships and what is learned in relationships. Carl Whitaker says that "psychotherapists

are susceptible to the disease of metacommunication"
(talking about talking). So, too, are ministers and
laypersons who, though they may no longer debate the
number of angels on the head of a pin, become enamored
of the latest jargon, theologies of liberation, conscious-
ness-raising, or what have you. I agree with Whitaker that
this can lead to a loss of caring, whether as a family
member or counselor or church person.

So what is needed, we believe, is not a book in which we
talk about talking or theorize about theories, but one in
which we reflect about living in families. What helps and
what hurts persons in their lives together as marriage
partners and family members? And how can the church,
and in particular its leaders, develop ways of enlivening
families to face the critical changes in today's society? And
how may families learn to help themselves use the support
of the values and traditions of the church?

Gail Sheehy, in *Passages*, looks at the ways individuals
must face the life stages of adulthood with the crises that
middle age, career change, widowhood, or divorce bring,
but from a secular point of view. The church needs to be
similarly aware of these changes both within the setting of
marriage and the family and in the context of faith.

What is the purpose of another book on family life and
family therapy? Although theory should not predominate,
there is a need to analyze the trouble in American families,
in particular the breakdown in their socializing function.
Why are families today not preparing their members to
relate to the larger community? Why are they not
imparting the traditions and values of the faith so that
children and young people have something on which to
center their lives and to serve as an anchor against the
swirling changes going on around them? More directly,
why is the church failing to make a connection with its
families in the critical period of child-rearing and
socializing? And why are families outside the church

failing to see the church as having anything to offer, even though parents flounder in despair and their children seek spiritual comfort in cultish religions and pop therapies?

I think another book needs to be written to alert ministers and church leaders to the systems approach and to marriage and family life. One needs to see the roots of family life whether in rural or urban or suburban North America.[1] The systems approach links together theory and practical experience in family living in an understandable way; role relationships and community support are not only perceived but made available for change and growth. Where there is breakdown in family life it is important to have some way of knowing what has gone wrong, and to help parents, children, and youth regain problem-solving abilities and some sense of equilibrium in their life together. Religious tradition and values are not to be thrown out but reevaluated and made contemporary for each family member. The church should not be at the periphery of this struggle but at its heart, and involved in supportive, caring, and strengthening ways. In facing these difficulties the central question is often not the *why* but the *what* and the *how*. So learning methods of family counseling, analyzing family problems, and seeing the whole family picture in the emerging world of the last decades of this century becomes an important task. The church *is* a community of communities when families see their socializing and enabling roles at work. In the following pages I enlist you, your family, and your koinonia group in the struggle to make of the family a strong place for growing love in this day.

I am dedicating the book to students with whom I have worked over the past twenty-five years. It has been an exciting period of learning for those of us working in family counseling. Some students have themselves become leaders, establishing counseling centers, experimenting and publishing. Others are using their knowledge and skills in parishes with families in the United States and abroad. In particular, I am grateful to classes in marriage and family counseling at Perkins, Princeton, and Wesley seminaries who have helped me focus this manuscript through lectures and case studies. The counselors whom I have supervised over the past twelve years at Baltimore and Washington Pastoral Counseling Centers have sharpened my clinical insight. I have benefitted by taking the family psychotherapy course in the department of psychiatry of Georgetown University (1978–79) while developing systems concepts. Then, I want to thank Beth Hampden, M.S.W., of Groome Child Guidance Center, who read the manuscript during its production and has improved its quality through her helpful critique. Mrs. Betty Haynes not only typed the entire manuscript but improved its reading quality through correcting my rough copy. Finally, I am continually grateful to my wife, Alma, who has shared marriage and has nurtured our family for thirty years and who, through long walks and talking with me while I have been writing, has made this more of a human document.

CHARLES WILLIAM STEWART

Chapter I

Trouble in the American Family

It doesn't take a social scientist to tell you that there is trouble in the American family. Mr. and Mrs. American Citizen pick up the morning newspaper and perceive that the conflicts they experience in their family are writ large in the problems about which they read. The statistics leap out at the reader. Divorce has become pandemic. From 1970 to 1975 the number of divorces has risen from 5.5% to 8.7% among white families. Among black families the statistics are higher. In the same period the number of divorces among blacks has risen from 19.9% to 26.6%. One-sixth of all children in this country live in one-parent families. Looked at another way, the number of children living with both parents has diminished from 85% in 1970 to 83% in 1975.

Today, many young adults are opting not to marry but to remain single. To speak statistically, the number of single persons between 25 and 34 has jumped about 50% between 1970 and 1975—from 2.8 million to 4.2 million. Many of these young adults are either living with one another without benefit of clergy or opting for other life-styles—single apartments, homosexual unions, living in communes—which do not involve the bearing or raising of children.[1]

Adolescent suicide and delinquency have risen, particularly among middle-class suburban youth. Junior and

13

senior high school youth[2] are vandalizing schools and getting involved in petty crime. Suicide among adolescents is a fairly recent phenomenon. O.D.s (drug overdose), suicide, auto accidents, or other violent acts represent cries for help among young people who feel they are not capable of coping with the demands of an adult society or feel starved for love and support from their parents.

Child beating and wife beating, crimes once kept away from the eyes of the community, now make the daily paper and weekly news supplements. To read about such matters makes us sick, but we need to know that in 1976 it was reported that 200,000 children were injured by their parents and that 2,000 of them died as a result of injuries.[3] Violence once associated with lower-class families and reported by police and hospital emergency units is coming from middle-class homes. Wife beating, like rape, is a crime against women's wills. The causes are hard to fathom—is it a product of the violence on television and in movies and paperback novels, as Frederic Wertham claims, or is it the result of frustration and boredom and loveless homes, something fundamentally wrong in family life?

There is a tear in the fabric of family life in America, which these statistics reflect only on the surface. It runs wide and it runs deep. In an interview with Susan Byrne, Urie Bronfenbrenner claims that Americans have been so busy doing their own thing that "fewer and fewer parents are doing their job of caring for children."[4] Children and youth are left to fend for themselves not only in ghettos but in suburbs with no baby sitter but the television set. (How many reruns of "Father Knows Best" can kids watch?) Left to their own devices, these children are not socialized, i.e., they have few role models upon which to pattern their lives and little stimulation to learn and to grow in their persons and characters. We have known since Durkheim and Freud that anomie and poor family cohesion are the seedbed for antisocial behavior, emotional disturbance, and suicide. The generation gap is then not simply the result of poor communication between parents and child but the outcome of parental absence from the home, failure to teach the child values for living, and an unwillingness to adapt individual life-styles to the cooperative structure necessary for the family.

Despite the troubles in the family, there is no danger of its dying. Margaret Mead, after a lifetime of studying families in all parts of the planet, concludes that "everywhere life within a family is the recognized way for a child to be reared." And, "as far back as our knowledge takes us," she says, "human beings have lived in families. We know of no period when this was not so. We know of no people who have succeeded for long in dissolving the family or displacing it. Instead men have exercised their imaginations in the elaboration of different styles of family living and different ways of relating the family to the larger community."[5]

History has recorded changes in the family from the three-generational (extended) form in primitive nomadic and agricultural settings to the small independent (nuclear) unit in industrial and urban complexes. Marital combinations from polygamy to monogamy (and even polyandry) have meant different ways of blending parents with children, but generally one male has been responsible for one family unit although his responsibilities may have extended to other kinfolk in the community. In North America with its pluralistic cultures one may find traditional family units among ethnic communities in Canada and the United States, and generally in Mexico and in rural parts of the continent. However, the small independent family has been the ideal, and families moving from the country to the city have pulled up their family roots, forsaken their neighborhoods, and traded the security of the farm, small town, and reservation for the attraction of the large city with its ghettos, high-rise apartments, and independent but rootless existence.

Broken homes, one-parent families, urban and suburban delinquency, battered children and wives, and a breakdown of sexual mores are the results. Our culture runs the risk of producing a generation of young adults who cannot build stable homes. Can we ask the state to take over the entire responsibility for families through its welfare programs and adoption/foster care practices? Or should we expect social workers and family therapists to be the solvers of family problems when the community is not doing long-range planning for healthy family life and individuals are confused as to just how to go about getting their own families in balance?

There is reason to be anxious about the family. Do you remember watching the documentary of the Loud family on television, to see an average kinship group (but certainly above average in income and life-style) play out their problems before the cameras? And do you recall how shocked you were to hear later that this family disintegrated as the father and mother sought a divorce over those same problems? Something is just not working in the independent family unit. *My thesis is that the nuclear family unit is too small, too isolated, and too lacking in roots and support systems to carry the total responsibility for sustaining parents and children today.* True, as the sociologists and anthropologists will tell you, the family is the unit par excellence for the bearing and rearing of children. But in moving from the traditional, neighborhood-oriented, father-dominated family to the modern, urban-oriented, and child-dominated family, the family ship has lost its rudder. And it is listing badly in many parts of the world.

What is the family's essential purpose? With some wit, Reuben Hill states:

Its (the family's) curious age and sex composition make it an inefficient work group, a poor planning committee, an unwieldy play group, and a group of uncertain congeniality. Its leadership is shared by two relatively inexperienced amateurs for the most of their incumbency, new to roles of spouse and parents. They must work with a succession of disciples having few skills and lacking in judgment under conditions which never seem to remain stable long enough to bring a settled organization. . . . Yet despite these disruptive features families manage to maintain, somehow, the structured interaction patterns that keep them viable.[6]

Urie Bronfenbrenner suggests that we don't need a new social vehicle. "All we need do is to create conditions to enable families to do what they do better than anyone else."[7] What is that? Biologically, the family is the best place for children to be conceived, born or adopted, and given physical care during their dependent years. Psychologically, the family is still the best unit for teaching a child the mother tongue, helping the child to learn what it is to be a person and how to live with others in a social unit, what the values of the culture are, and how to adapt to those values. Sociologically, the family is the best place to learn what marriage and family life are all about, and to begin to make the first overtures into the wider community of school, work, and citizenship.

The family is a flexible unit, but one which attempts to maintain a haven and a base from which its members may negotiate the changes necessary for survival in the wider society. When people are caught in such fast-moving and revolutionary times as they have been in this century, is it any wonder that the family base feels the full impact of those changes? We have advocated changes in the traditional family structure in order that families may move to the cities to work in the offices and factories and to enable them to gain a better standard of living, education, health care, and recreation. But the nuclear family (the small independent family) living unto itself apart from the background and roots from which it came is the unit which is threatened today. What has been lost along with the traditional family structure is the contributions of the older generation, the support system of neighborhood, the teaching of family traditions, and the possibility of the family cooperating as a viable work unit. While in many instances the family has gained economically, it has failed to better itself as a viable social unit. One father who had worked his way through high school and college and now insisted that his sons not work while in college said, "I don't know *when* they will learn to work." And another father said, "I've made things good for them, but I haven't made them better."

The nuclear family has kept the male in a dominant position and has not allowed for a structure which makes for coequal status of women with men. In a day of psychologists and child specialists, parents have become confused about their natural roles as care-givers to their children and often have given up in confusion and despair. When religious beliefs and moral codes broke down for many families, they did not find help from the clergy or from the church. Pragmatic philosophies, self-realization psychologies, and situation ethics have been grasped at to fill the breach but have often been found lacking in the face of revolutionary change.

Needed are new family forms commensurate with the new challenges confronting us in the society. Needed are new ways for families to meet crises and to find the roots of their lives together. Needed are new care and support structures—which may hark back to neighborhoods and communities of a former day but which will enable the small nuclear structure to find larger ground upon which to sink its little foundation. The Christian faith espouses that God has created women and men to live together in families and that the rearing of children is a Christian vocation. We must not be discouraged, therefore, when it appears that the ways we knew as children appear not to be teachable to our children. Families have experienced this phenomenon in rapidly changing societies in all periods of history.

So, I would invite you to investigate your roots and the ground from which you were digged, in the following pages. Through this discussion I would hope you might understand the roles, relationships and systems which make up family life. And with this background, I would encourage you then to investigate the crises which occur in family life, what makes for them and how family members may resolve them. As a counselor or as one who goes to a counselor, you are then invited to understand the counseling process, particularly from a *faith* or *church* point of view. If you are involved in counseling you are then invited to understand the family nature of the church, and some of the newer ways of building family support structures within neighborhood groups.

We should not lose heart for, as Voltaire might be paraphrased, if the family did not exist we should have to invent it. Our basic theological belief is that the family is the creation of God, even though its forms are man's invention. We need to be imaginative and insightful so that through our prayerful thought and mature action the family might not just survive, but that we may find ways in which each member may realize his[8] full humanity and be enabled to enter into loving relationships with others.

Chapter II
The Roots of the Family

The family as a form is safe. But particular changes—changes that take country people into city tenements, immigrants across the seas, and young people to places where they lack the help traditionally given them by their elders—cause hardships, especially for those who are the pioneers in a new family form.

—Margaret Mead[1]

The interest in Alex Haley's best seller, *Roots*, springs not only from the average American's concern about black history and black culture before, during, and after the Civil War, but also from the fundamental desire to understand "the pit from which we were digged." Rootless Americans want to know their origins, but more fundamentally they want to become rooted. The search for roots is the search for identity (Who am I?). It is also the search for relatedness (To what do I belong? What are my foundations?).

Let's begin by looking at the family to get some idea about its shape and contour. What gives a family its identity? How does the individual develop his sense of place and rootedness within the family? Using my own family tree as illustration, I want to explain what is inherent in *generations:* how the sins of the fathers, and also the virtues and vocations of parents, are visited "to children unto the third and fourth generations." Then I want to investigate some representative American families where patterns of rootedness may be reflected. With these empirical materials we may then ask: What are the problems of both rootlessness and rootedness in American society? What helps and hinders families in developing the cohesiveness, flexibility, and capacity to maintain themselves in the midst of vast social change which groups are experiencing in this century? Finally, we shall hope to arrive at some definition of what it means for a family to be firmly rooted, a mature and growing social unity.

1. Family Trees

One may define the family as those persons related by blood, marriage, or adoption who live under one roof or in one compound. However, this would miss the dynamic elements of family life. The family is a system or network of roles (mother-father-son-daughter) formed from the images and behaviors which grow out of continuing relationships. The family of origin is the family from which one springs—one's parents one generation back. The primary family is the family which one establishes upon marriage or agreement to live together. The purpose of the family is to bring forth the next generation and to raise it to maturity. More personally, families are places where persons can share closeness, companionship, and love.

The primary learning within the family is social learning. There is a need to learn social roles. "The need is to become and remain an accepted and respected, differentiated and integrated part of a congenial, functioning group, the collective purposes of which are congruent with the individual's ideals."[2] The child learns what it is to be a boy or a girl by identifying with the sexual role of the parent of the same sex and through absorbing the family system into his own organism. This is what makes individuals human—the family context in which they grow up. The *rootedness* of an individual means he has a *place*, a geographical place he calls home. And *home*, Robert Frost says, is "the place where, when you have to go there, they have to take you in." This is soil in which the family tree takes root. To be rootless is to give this up, to pull it up or not to become rooted in the first place. Abused or battered children will choose to go back to their parents who have hurt them rather than go to a foster home where they will not be abused. This is where their roots are; why shouldn't they want to?

Some persons will have traced their family tree through genealogical study as a way of discovering who their ancestors were and where they came from. Family systems psychotherapists have developed a method called the *genogram* as a means of taking a family history, but with the possibility of uncovering some previously hidden information and unconscious connections between the generations. Guerin calls a genogram

a structural diagram of a family's generational relationship system. . . . This diagram is a roadmap of the family relationship system. Once the names, the age of each person, the dates of marriages, death, divorces and births are filled in, other pertinent facts about the relationship process can be gathered, including the family's physical location, frequency and type of contact, emotional cutoffs, toxic issues, nodal events, and open/closed relationship index.[3]

Let me illustrate by using my own family as an example: Both my parents came from rural areas in eastern Ohio. At ages twenty and eighteen they met at normal school, where they studied for teaching certificates. They were separated for two years during World War I; and, when my father returned, they were married in 1920 and settled on the "lower place" on my grandfather's farm. Following my birth, in 1921, mother and father decided to go back into teaching and moved to a small suburb of Wheeling, West Virginia, in eastern Ohio. A daughter was born in 1923. My father accepted the principalship of a private school in 1926, where he remained until his retirement in 1964. My mother taught as a substitute teacher during my boyhood and taught full time at my father's school after I went to college. Both parents were educated in extension classes, my father receiving his B.A. in 1946.

My mother came from a large family, being the oldest of eight children. My father came from a family of three, being the youngest and only son. Besides farming, both grandfathers were lay preachers. Our family was close to

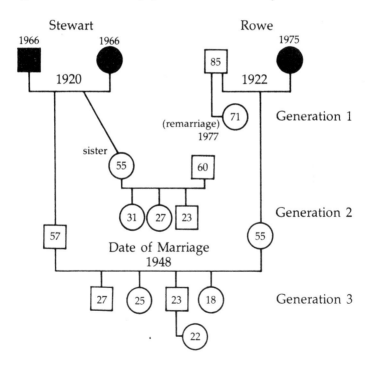

both grandparents and went to visit them on the farms during vacations and holidays. However, when my father's parents died, my sister and I drifted away from his side of the family. My mother's family has always been more strongly connected. When my grandmother and grandfather divorced, two of the younger "boys" went back to the farm to live and take care of my grandmother. When she died, my mother was the "head of the family" and, since her death, my oldest aunt has assumed that position, arranging for family reunions and keeping in touch with us all.

My sister, Anne, met her husband in Puerto Rico, where she went as a teacher in a mission school. He is the oldest child in a minister's family, and was serving as a career officer until his retirement. She resumed teaching in Germany after the birth of her last child. She has since obtained a master's degree and works as a reading specialist in the university town in which they reside.

My wife, Alma, is an only child. Her parents come from New England and met on a farm in Maine, where her mother visited and her father worked during the summer. They were married in 1922, after World War I and a long engagement. They settled first in New York City, but moved in 1924 to a farm in Massachusetts. Her father is college educated in horticulture, and her mother attended secretarial school. They moved to various cities during World War II following war-time jobs, but returned to live out their lives on the family farm following the war.

Alma and I met at Union Seminary in New York City in 1946 and were married in 1948. I am an ordained United Methodist minister and, after serving churches while studying for the doctorate, have been a theological school teacher all my professional life. Alma served as a Director of Christian Education before our marriage. She secured a master's degree in library science in 1971 and has worked at a private girls' school since our older son has gone to college.

Three of our children were born while were were in the

parish, and the last after I went to my first teaching post. The oldest, a son, twenty-seven, has a master's degree in business administration and is in business. A daughter, twenty-five, works as an elementary school teacher; and the second son, twenty-four, as a musical instructor in a high school. The youngest, a daughter, eighteen, is in high school. They are very close to one another, having spent a great deal of time together at church camps and with us on family vacations during the time they were growing up. The older son has been closest to Alma's parents, going to the family farm as I did in the summer. The older daughter is close to my sister's daughter, who lives near us and has a child whom Louise babysits. The younger two are friendly to both sides of the family. My sister, Anne, and I have become closer since we moved to the same part of the country, and since our parents' deaths in 1966.

Alma's mother died at our home just before Thanksgiving, 1975. This was a shock for all of us, but one which brought us close together. Her father, a very independent person, did not want to leave the farm. He continued to live there alone for nearly two years, socializing with friends and neighbors and spending winters in Florida. He and a close friend were married in October of 1977. She is also a gardener and a widow with two married children and two grandchildren. My wife, an only child, now has a larger family than she has ever experienced before.

What are the generational patterns observable in my family? The move from farm (Gen. 1) to small town (Gen. 2) to city and suburb (Gen. 3) is quite evident. The farms on which my grandparents lived are no longer economically operable, and my wife's father's farm is now just a leisure-time activity. Education became the means on both sides of the family by which members could advance themselves, professionally and economically. Teaching as a profession has been passed on from my parents' generation to my generation and now to our children. The church also has been prominent in both my mother's family and my father's. I went into the ministry and my sister into mission service as a direct influence of my parents, and for me the influence of my grandfather was also a factor.

My family is a nuclear family with extensive connections to my mother's family, my sister's family, and to my wife's father and his wife. The loosening of connections to my father's family was not intentional but came largely after we moved away from rural Ohio and to Eastern cities. Our difference in education has futher set us apart. When my parents died, my sister and I then became the older generation (with the exception of my wife's father). The fact that three of our children have not yet married tends to keep the family connected. We still spend holidays and vacations together, but now girl friends and boy friends are included in the family.

2. Six Families

In this section we want to look at short case histories of six families—studied in depth by film and by interview[4]— which should allow us to see the ways in which the culture of America has been transmitted from generation to generation. We want then to apply the following questions about the search for roots to each family.

(1) What are the connections of the family members to one another? How are the grandparents related to the parents? And how are the parents related to the children? Is there a family tree in the sense that the family is not cut off from other family members but is rooted back in the parents' and grandparents' generations?

(2) What is the family's sense of place? Is the family rooted in an area? Or have they moved about from one area to another so that one could say that they are uprooted or, in fact, rootless? This gets at mobility within the family.

(3) What is the family's sense of tradition? Are they rooted in a faith and in values which they transmit to their children? Or have they broken away from the family traditions so that they no longer practice a faith or live by ethical standards which were transmitted to them by their parents?

(4) Does the family know when to plant and when to pluck up (Ecclesiastes 3)? Is the family over-rooted to the point that traditions or socioeconomic situations prevent them from growing and developing the full potential of each family member? Does the family allow for individual growth? Is the family flexible and capable of change in the midst of crisis? Jesus' parables of growth included the parable of the vine which needed grafting and pruning but which was rooted for several seasons and the parable of the mustard seed which grew for only a season, then seeded itself and died in order to be planted in another place.

Seventy-five years ago three-quarters of all Americans lived on the land. Today, 4 percent farm. The Stephens family is part of that minority. Carl, fifty, and Lois, forty-nine, own 360 acres and rent 450 more near Villisca, Iowa. The land has been in Lois' family for more than a century.

Four children—Marc, sixteen; Cecil, fourteen; Martha, twelve; and Mary, nine—live at home. Two older children are married. Marie, twenty-five, lives on a nearby farm with her husband, Bill, and their two youngsters. Howard, twenty-three, was a hired hand on his parents' farm when the film was made. He and his wife, Janell, a practical nurse (as is Marie), live in a house trailer.

Thrift and hard work are necessary to make ends meet on the Stephens place. Everyone works. Martha can drive a tractor. Farming is a high-risk, expensive undertaking that often yields minimum financial return. Producers of food pit their labor against possible bad weather and low prices. The costs of fertilizer, equipment and fuel keep increasing. Carl and Lois are a hundred thousand dollars in debt; cash income has averaged six thousand dollars in recent years. While there is time for recreation when chores are done, it is easy to understand why formal vacations are not in the budget. Activities center around farm, school, and church. The family attends the First Christian Church of Carinda.

Carl and Lois' greatest pride is their children, all of whom love the land, respect nature, and are willing to work. They consider their life good, safe, and meaningful. Yet the elder Stephenses, like many farm couples, feel uneasy. They see family farming and rural values threatened in an overwhelmingly urban society. "I think the city folk just don't understand what farming is," Carl says.

"The Pasciaks, like many ethnic families, find themselves in two worlds," Paul Wilkes writes. Stanley and Lorraine, the parents, are second generation Polish-Americans reared in patterns brought from the old country. They grew up in a Polish neighborhood only a mile from where they now live on Chicago's South Side.

The Pasciak children know a more open society. Despite the ethnic heritage kept alive in home and church (Five Holy Martyrs Roman Catholic parish), they are less interested in Polish customs. Gerard, seventeen, a musician, sums it up when he says he has no intention of becoming the next "polka king."

Carol, twenty-three, the oldest child, is married and has worked since graduation from high school. She and Tom, her Italian-American husband, live near her parents, but they skip out early on the family Christmas Eve festivities. Gary, twenty-one, was home from Southern California for Christmas when the film was shot. His pursuit of an acting career is a major theme and cause of tension. The younger children are Patrick, fifteen; Tom, fourteen; and Maryann, eleven.

Stanley Pasciak is a roughhewn, gentle man. He is a

foreman in the Chicago Department of Sanitation. Petite Lorraine cleans offices at night. Her real vocation is motherhood. All Pasciaks are raised to work, and everyone at home has a paying job, even Maryann. Gary's determination to follow his own career inclinations is in sharp contrast to his parents' understanding of work and their concept of family solidarity.

When Jackie Katz took a job instead of marrying straight out of college her parents worried—unnecessarily. "I was born and bred to be married," says Jackie, the child of a Chicago Jewish family. Jackie fantasized her husband as a sensitive, attractive lawyer. They would live in San Francisco and have two children. One day it happened. She met Arne Greenberg, lawyer, living in San Francisco, home to Chicago for a wedding.

Jackie and Arne, married in 1960, bought a showcase home north of the Golden Gate and set out to achieve the American dream of prosperity and happiness. Fifteen years and two children (a third was lost to crib death) later, they were divorcing. Prosperity they had. Happiness eluded what seemed an ideal couple. Marriage was not what they expected.

Jackie and the children—Michael, twelve, and Mari, nine—represent a single-parent family still involved with the second parent.

Jackie likes a balanced room, a balanced life, but something was badly out of balance in her marriage. Jackie is an attentive mother, but she is lonely. Arne obviously cares deeply for Michael and Mari and has them some weekends. Mari clearly dislikes her parents' separation but is less traumatized than is Michael. Jackie and Arne want a compatible divorce. Yet before the decree is final, they are squabbling over schedules and discipline involving the children. The Greenbergs were always going to discuss problems later. For their marriage, "later" came too late.

Robert and Peggy George are upwardly mobile black Americans. They and their three teen-aged children live in Laurelton, a quiet semi-suburban community in Queens, a borough of New York City.

Thirty-nine-year-old Bob, an ex-Marine, is assigned as a policeman to a precinct in Bedford-Stuyvesant, Brooklyn's vast, volatile ghetto. Peggy works as a supervisor in a large insurance company office and also carries the responsibilities of "housewife." The children—Karen, seventeen; Debbie, fifteen; and Derek, thirteen—are in school.

The Georges "are and are not part of the middle class," Paul Wilkes says in his book, *Six American Families*. With their own home, two cars, and an income of $32,000 they are financially middle class, "but because they are black they also know about second-class citizenship." Sensitive to the subtle ties of racism and conscious of growing "black pride," neither Bob nor Peggy nor their children are militantly black. They, like countless other ethnic minority families, willingly pursue the American dream. While spotlighting particular concerns of blacks in the mid-seventies, the George film makes it clear that middle-income American families of all races share many of the same challenges. Asked why her family did the film, Peggy replied, "It would give white America a chance to see how blacks, or some blacks, live . . . that we're striving for the same thing they are."

Nancy Kennedy is an attractive, alert seventeen-year-old high school senior convinced she is a born loser. Her self-assessment surprises her father, Jim, epitome of the American overachiever. Joan (Mrs. Kennedy) says little as her husand and daughter spar over the marks of success. Joan is unsure of the extent of her capabilities, although she is a confident and patient mother to David, a twelve-year-old mongoloid, and Tracy, a four-year-old adopted daugher.

Joan and Jim, both forty years old, and the two oldest

children are midwestern transplants to Albuquerque. Jim, a Ph.D. in chemical engineering, is one of five thousand men and women responsible for the development and design of the U.S. arsenal of nuclear weapons. Joan stays home—too much, she is beginning to think, especially since David is in a special education program and Tracy in nursery school. She has never worked except for four years in an office while Jim was in college, before their marriage.

Nancy is a better than average student and plans to go to college, perhaps to prepare herself to work with retarded children like her brother. David is doing well learning basic skills. He attends a good school, and the fact that his needs are being met while others with similar handicaps are neglected has turned his father into a crusader. Jim Kennedy is a prime mover in a class action suit seeking to force New Mexico to upgrade programs for all handicapped persons. The Kennedys are active Lutherans.

The Burks are a clan. Grace and Arlon, seven of their ten living children, four in-laws, and eight grandchildren share a five-acre tract in a hollow beyond the Dalton city dump. Three other children and their families live nearby. Everyone is in and out of Grace's small house—literally hers, as she owns the property—almost every day. Livelihoods come mainly from low-paying jobs in carpet mills in the hill country of north Georgia.

All three generations reflect what sociologists call a "culture of poverty," a cycle of economic, educational, and social deprivation hard to break. The Burks do not want to be poor. They are proud people who refuse welfare. They simply do not know how to escape poverty, so they accept it. Yet readers must not let poverty blind them to the Burks as individuals and as people of joy, courage, and down-to-earth wisdom. This family need feel no shame.

Grace, fifty-five, the backbone of the clan, was for years the major breadwinner, despite having thirteen children.

Arlon, sixty-five, held manual labor jobs but was often ill, and drinking did not help his work record. The parents now receive $128 a month from Social Security. Three children—Ruby, fifteen; Thomas, twenty; and James Earl, seventeen—live with Grace and Arlon. The sons pay some room and board.

Two other small houses and two house trailers cluster around the parents' house. Mary, thirty, and Peggy, eighteen, their husbands (who are brothers), and children have the houses. One trailer is occupied by James Arlon, Jr., thirty-five, Willie Mae, and two youngsters; the other by Jean, thirty-four, her husband, and two children. Charlotte, twenty-two; Charles, twenty-eight; and William, twenty-nine; and their families are close by.

Three sons are dead—one in infancy, two by violence. One was killed by a shotgun blast and the other when he and buddies escaped from reform school. Four sons have spent some time in jail.

Now let us apply the questions posed on pages 26-27 to these six families. First, what are the connections of the family members to one another? In two instances we notice that family connections are firm and that these extend over several generations—in particular, the Stephens family and the Burk family. The Stephens family is rooted in the land, and their family members help make a living on that land. The Burk family has a clan kind of family arrangement centered around the mother and the family tract upon which the various homes have been built and settled upon. The Pasciak family and the George family are ethnic families which have previously had strong family ties but in which the connections are now loosening. The Greenbergs and Kennedy families have both migrated from their Midwestern origins. Although they maintain connection with the grandparents, this is largely confined to holiday periods.

Second, what is the family's sense of place? Is the family

rooted in an area, or have they moved about from one area to another? Again, the Stephens and Burk families are deeply rooted in a geographical place. The Burk family, I would say, are overrooted in their family compound. It is difficult to see how they could possibly move anywhere else. The second generation has stayed in or near the family place, and they come back to the mother's house when they are in difficulty or need to be bailed out of trouble. The Stephens family live on the same farm on which the mother was brought up, and their children are expected to root themselves in this family farm. However, one can see the necessity for the older son to take a factory job because of the difficulty in buying land and in making a living on a small, independent family farm.

The other families are not as firmly rooted in a place. The Pasciak family has settled in a Polish neighborhood, but the children are beginning to move away from this neighborhood in search of larger horizons. The George family has moved away from the inner city to the suburbs, and their place is more tentative, although they are rooted in their racial connections. The Greenberg and Kennedy families have both moved to new places, away from their families of origin. They have set down roots in new communities, but one gets the impression that they would move tomorrow to follow their work. In fact, the separation in the Greenberg family is causing a sense of uprootedness for Arne, the father.

Third, what is the family's sense of tradition? Are they rooted in a faith and in a value system which they transmit to their children? The three church families are the Pasciak family, the Kennedy family, and the Stephens family. The Kennedys and the Stephenses are white Anglo-Saxon Protestant. Their ethic is the Protestant work ethic, and their tradition is the mainline Protestant tradition. In both instances the parents are teaching the children the Protestant tradition and work ethic. The Pasciak family is rooted in the traditional faith and values of the Roman Catholic church plus the Polish tradition (language, dancing, music, and so on). The children are breaking away from the Polish traditions, marrying outside the Polish group, and seeking their fortunes in the larger world. The Greenberg and George families are ethnic families which have attempted to transcend their origins. The Greenbergs have uprooted themselves and are not firmly based in the religion and ethic of their families of origin. The George family has also been uprooted and does not participate in the black church but does find their home within the folkways and mores of black people. The Burk family is also unchurched and engages in a survival ethic and clan loyalty. The mother's strength sustains them in the face of crisis, loss of job, going to jail, and so forth.

Fourth, is the family flexible so that there is allowance for individual growth and change in the midst of crisis? The most flexible family is the Greenberg family. The parents have engaged in the study of various popular psychologies in order to help them attain individual self-fulfillment. However, there is a lack of flexibility within the family system, which shows itself in the problems between Arne and Jackie eventuating in the separation and divorce. The George family is fairly flexible. They have moved out of the inner city and into the middle-class suburb. The Kennedy family is not as flexible as one might think at the outset. The family has faced the problems accompanying the birth of a mongoloid son well, but the wife feels she has been bound to a homemaker and child-care role overly long. The older daughter is feeling the pressure of the father's expectations, and the father is not facing up to his need to spend more time with the family—all of which reflect inflexibility. The least flexible appear to be the Stephens family, the Pasciak family, and the Burk family. Mr. Stephens appears to be least flexible, with the second generation having to become freed up from the family farm and consider the wider world around them. The Pasciak family is in a similar situation, with Mrs. Pasciak rather inflexible and the children having to fight for independence outside the Polish Catholic neighborhood in which they were reared. The Burk family is perhaps the most static; they are determined in their lives by the fact that they are caught in a cycle of poverty. They are therefore unable to do anything other than what they do, and the men's alcoholism and the women's drudgery are reinforced by poor diet, inadequate education, and jobs at the lowest level of income.

3. Patterns of Rootedness

We want now to look at how both individuals and total families relate to the societies of which they are a part. First, what are the patterns by which individuals relate to the culture? In the first section we observed the powerful socializing agency of the family through the generations. Is it possible to look now in more detail at those patterns which set individuals and families apart from another?

Kluckhohn and Murray say that most individuals are "culture carriers or conservers. There are also culture creators, destroyers and disintegrators. . . . One function of personality is to transform itself as far as possible in the direction of identifying with both the conserving and creative forces in humanity."[5] Personality, therefore, is the product of the individual's adaptation of his drives and needs systems to the demands of the social group. This adaptation may be *oversocialized*, meaning that the individual develops neurotic defenses and is hampered in his creativity. The adaptation may be *undersocialized*, meaning that the individual releases his aggression against social institutions and may need to be controlled by those who protect society against criminal elements and lawbreakers. Or the individual may be able to balance his needs and drives against the demands of the society and is termed an adequately socialized and functioning social number.

What are the patterns of relationship between a family and a culture? David Riesman, in *The Lonely Crowd*, analyzes ways in which families have adapted to the demands of the society. These are represented by the traditional, the inner-directed, and the other-directed orientations. The traditional orientation is one in which the family is established around a tradition. Generally the father is the head of the family, the mother is the nurturer and care-giver, and the children are extensions of the parents. The tradition may be religious or ethical, but it also involves many family customs. These are taught around the hearth, and the tendency is for the family to be rooted in the soil and oriented toward conserving the heritage of the past. The inner-directed family is oriented around conscience and the obeying of the inner call to work, thrift, and doing one's duty to family members. Children are expected to succeed in their school work, their athletic contests, and to become upward-mobile within the society. Production and achievement are learned within the family system so that the family members can produce and achieve outside in the industrial-business complex. The other-directed family, first analyzed in the fifties, is directed by a radar system sensitive to what others of one's social group expected it to be. The mass media are the taste-setters, and the family is oriented toward consuming the goods and services supplied by an expanding economy. With increasing leisure, work is not important except as it provides the means whereby one can consume more. Keeping up with the Joneses and being sensitive to what peers think of one become more important than conscience or tradition.

Since Riesman's analysis, Kenneth Keniston and others have attempted to understand youth and young adults of the late sixties and seventies who protested the materialism and wastefulness of the American society and showed their alienation by active protest, by dropping out of college and the establishment of business and work, and by attempting to foster simpler life-styles. Oscar Lewis coined the term "culture of poverty," and Michael Harrington[6] and others have studied the more than 50 million Americans who live below the poverty level. They are victims of unemployment and are locked into inadequate housing, nourishment, and education. They also lack other means whereby they might break out of the depressed and depressing conditions in which they live.

Sociologists also point out that in the last century in the United States many families have moved from an extended kind of organization (multiple generations which live together, work together, and maintain their connections over the years) toward nuclear families (one generation which lives to itself and is separate from the family of origin). In addition, one must factor in the one-parent families, couples who live together without marrying, and the singles of the same sex who may live together, some of whom have foster children or children born out of wedlock. As more and more families have moved away from the farm and small town into the city and suburb, the connections with the family of origin have weakened. Many persons, not just the ethnic families, are what Margaret Mead calls "immigrant personalities." They are caught in a strange culture and are maladjusted without the roots of family tradition and customs which give them stability. They are "strangers in a strange land": blacks in a predominantly white society, farmers in a predominantly urban society, or those who practice a traditional religious faith and ethic in a predominantly secular society. As a matter of fact, Robert Lifton says that it is only the highly adaptable individual or family that is capable of living in such fluid and rapidly changing social conditions as those represented throughout the world today. *Protean* man, he says, is the one who realizes the irrelevance of old value systems and adapts by taking on new value systems in the cultures in which he is living.[7] One finds examples of this in the Jewish youth who converts to Hare Krishna or the Protestant youth who becomes a Zen Buddhist monk. In both instances there is a shift from the tradition of the past and a search for a new tradition which will help the individual find a faith and value system in which he is at home.

What are the patterns of rootedness in relationship to the families which we have been observing? There are first the *overly rooted*. These families not only have a sense of place but, for various reasons, have become so rooted that they are inflexible and have made it difficult for members of the family to move out of the family system. Second, there are the *thinly rooted*. These are the families who have found a place but have put down their roots tentatively with little depth. These are often upward mobile families who have moved from their families of origin and maintain few connections with relatives or friends of former years. More than likely these are nuclear families with few roots; these may also be extended families whose children are moving out from the family and are establishing residences in other areas. Third, there are the *uprooted*, the highly mobile families who have moved away from their families of origin, who maintain few connections with their family, and who do not form connections with members of their community. They are today's version of the gypsy. Finally, there are the *well-rooted*. These are families who are *autonomous*, and are the ones we shall be examining in the remaining chapters.

My thesis is that the nuclear family, particularly the family which is thinly rooted or uprooted, is the family which is in trouble today. The connections to family members, a sense of place, a sense of tradition, and some awareness of when to plant and when to pluck up lead members of a family to be firmly rooted. These characteristics are found in the earlier extended family but have deteriorated as more and more persons moved away from their families of origin and the communities and neighborhoods in which they came to maturity.

What are the problems raised by rootedness? From observing the six families one can draw the following conclusions:

(1) When survival is the primary focus, families tend to become overly rooted, with their members less flexible in relation to place, to work, and to moving out into the larger society. This is in evidence among the poor and among ethnics who have migrated from another land.

(2) Upward mobility may be related to the Protestant work ethic, but it also may be absorbed from the society in which families are placed. The work ethic and the drive for success and status may overly determine the family's activities. On the other hand, the work ethic, diffused by other-directed patterns of suburban families, may affect the relations of children to parents. This is particularly true when wives work outside the home. Thin-rootedness and a lack of family cohesiveness and family flexibility may be the result.

(3) Traditional families may have difficulty maintaining roots in a traditional faith and ethic, expressed in the conflict between the parents and children. The generation gap is built into the quality of many ethnic families rooted in a faith and tradition. Where parents attempt to continue outworn traditions, children may overtly or covertly rebel against traditional teaching.

(4) The connections of one family member to another suffer in urban and suburban surroundings. Lacking roots, and with few supportive family structures or neighbor-hoods to foster rootedness, the children of such families may become alienated from society. The kinds of problems represented by vandalism, escape through alcoholism and drug addiction, and other kinds of antisocial behavior are the result.

What helps and what hinders families in developing a sense of well-rootedness? We have discovered that rootedness depends upon (1) the family members' connectedness to one another (the intergenerational cohesiveness represented by a family tree); (2) the family's sense of place, in being planted in a geographical area, sufficiently so that it has a home and that home has an attraction for each family member; (3) a family tradition, a religious faith, a sense of values which are transmitted from parents to child, which tradition anchors that family against the crises and blows which come to it from outside; and (4) flexibility and freedom which allows individual family members to grow and to develop fully and for the family structure itself to change to allow such growth.

All families do not develop a sense of cohesiveness and flexibility in the same way. All families do not teach the values of the tradition or the cultural values in the same fashion. These values go through the highly personal grid of each particular family. One may conclude that there are no absolute norms for family life but that the norms relate to such factors as mentioned above: cohesiveness, flexibility, sense of place, and parents serving as transmitters of faith and value systems. These factors work within each family system, appropriate for each family in its context and for its particular life situation.

We may conclude that *rootedness is the capacity to sink deep within one's family tradition and values, to draw strength from the older generation, to maintain oneself in the face of stress, and to provide for the growth and self-fulfillment of each family member within the family system.* We should not think that the well-rooted family is an ideal type, transcending all American families, a dream which everyone is attempting to fulfill. The well-rooted family is rather the full-functioning family, with parents serving as adult guarantors of the children and youth in their care, teaching the values of its tradition but also able to change its own structure and way of functioning so that each family member may be able to become the whole person he has the possibility of becoming.

Now we want to look in more detail at the development of the family from the marriage of a man and a woman and the creation of a new family through the launch of the last child, and the change of family structure and functioning throughout one generation of family life. This will give us a dynamic look at the development of role relationships and family systems.

Exercises

(1) Make a genogram of your own family. What does it tell you about your socialization, development of vocation, and the roots of your values and traditions?

(2) View one or more of the Six Families films with your class or group, using the study guide to discuss the questions which are raised along with questions on pages 26-27 of this chapter.

Chapter III
The Family in Process

As American men and women attempt to shape new relationships, the family is being challenged as never before, from within as well as from without. Experts intensely debate the social implications of this dual challenge, with some envisioning the dawn of an enlightened, creative society while others are deeply disturbed by what they see as a loss of values, a burgeoning instability that may have dire consequences for democratic institutions. The new challenge and the new relationships that have spawned it have made this the age of the fragile family, the family in transition.

—Jon Nordheimer[1]

The family is in trouble, say some family sociologists and family psychotherapists. On the other side of the argument is Mary Jo Bane, a sociologist who began her research pessimistically but who changed her mind when she began to get her data together. She says:

The arguments predicting the imminent decline of the family seem to be supported by a good deal of statistical evidence: rising divorce rates, declining fertility rates, rising numbers of women leaving the home for paid work, diminution of the family's productive economic functions, the disappearance of the extended family. Yet as I delved further into the data that describe what Americans do and how they live, I became less sure that the family was in trouble. Surprising statistics showed up of the persistence of commitments to family life.[2]

The family is a complex interpersonal form which allows for both continuity and change. To gain a better perspective on the problems of the family, we want now, having examined the roots of family life, to look at the family as a social system. To understand the disturbances, conflicts, and crises of family life, we need first to understand its healthy functioning, from its beginnings with marriage to the launch of the final child. The relationships of the family represent the continuities; but the family grows and develops and is a process as well as a continuity. It can work poorly and need help from outside; but it can work fairly well, with its members rising to challenges from within and without.

1. The Family as a System

Let's begin simply. A system is a "set of elements standing in interaction" (Bertalanffy, 1952). For example, the pump is a mechanical system made up of a piston, valves, a handle, and a spout connected to a stand of pipe. The parts interact and the pump works drawing water from a well. The human heart is a pump in a more complex physiological system made up of muscle, arteries, and veins interacting to circulate blood throughout the body. A woman and a man who marry establish a social system which at its simplest level is an interacting set of elements. The marriage and family (when children are born into it) are made more complex by the human factors of consciousness and self-determination. However, the circular interaction between wife and husband and between children and parents qualifies them as systems.

Let me state a series of axioms about the family as a system which will allow the reader to understand the systemic nature of the family:

1. Marital and family systems are working networks of relationships between husbands and wives and between parents and children.

2. Individuals have both intrapsychic needs and interpersonal needs which lead them to project role expectations upon marital partners and develop role behaviors within the institution called marriage. Similar expectations and behaviors developed around family members lead to family roles.

3. A homeostatic balance of needs is achieved and a contract formed when members communicate their needs and overtly or tacitly agree as to the functioning of the marriage and/or family system.

4. The marriage/family system changes as members grow, life situations alter, and the couple/family cycles through phases of development, necessitating new understanding of roles and new working out of contracts.

Interaction

Two people who relate at any level of intensity attempt to influence each other. One sees this when John, having been attracted by Mary at a party, decides to get acquainted. They set up a pattern of communication using words, facial

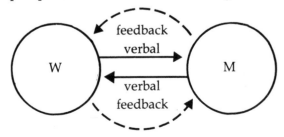

expressions, and body gestures which get their "message" across. They not only speak but they listen to one another and give feedback both verbally and nonverbally to what they hear from the other.

Suppose that John asks Mary to go to the corner drive-in after the party for refreshments and further conversation. His action is met by a positive reaction from Mary, and a beginning system is formed.

Don Jackson explains:

According to the systems concept, a change occurs when related parts are rearranged be they atoms or the behavior of closely associated human beings, such as two people who are married. . . . The systems concept makes it clear that a change in the behavior of one spouse is usually a reaction to changes in his partner's behavior, and in turn causes additional change in the partner's behavior. This action-reaction system operates in a circular fashion (sometimes vicious, sometimes positive).[3]

Role Relationship

To leap ahead to the point where John and Mary decide to get married, we may further understand the elements of a marital system. Both John and Mary have intrapsychic and interpersonal needs. The intrapsychic needs are historically more primitive: the need to be fed and to be soothed when anxious, the need for sexual gratification, the need for shelter and the warmth of clothing and fire, the need for a place for things of one's own. Interpersonal needs are more recent in human evolution and draw one being to another being. Because human infants grow up in family units and other social units, they develop social needs in addition to intrapsychic needs. The need for companionship, for intimacy, for communication, and for the social ordering of one's work and play all develop as John and Mary grow to maturity within a family. Now they decide to form their own social unit or marital system. "To live in reasonable harmony the spouses negotiate with respect to their

behavior and responsibilities."[4] Jackson calls the product of
the negotiations a *quid pro quo* agreement (a something-for-
something agreement). That is, I am willing to give
something in order to get something. I have previously
called it a role-relationship based on expectations and
behavior agreed upon and negotiated. "A role is an
interpersonal relationship within a social system like the
family consisting of actor or ego and a social object or alter
ego. Role relationships are those demands which the actor
places upon a social object."[5] Thus John expects sexual
relations with Mary, and she is willing to give them. Mary
expects companionship and a sharing of household duties
and he accedes to them.

Homeostatic balance
of needs met

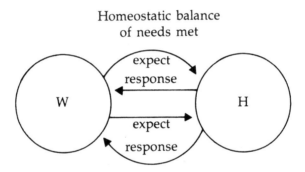

The marital role relationship comes into existence when
these expectations and reponses are commonly understood
by the marital partners and are built into their marital
relationship as rights and duties. Thus John's rights are
Mary's duties, and Mary's rights are John's duties.

At the interpersonal level the couple seeks homeostasis,
which is a balance in the satisfaction of their needs at various
levels: for food, sex, safety, security, love, children, and so
on. Virginia Satir explains: "According to the concept of
family homeostasis, the family acts so as to achieve a balance
in relationships. Members help to maintain their balance

overtly and covertly. The family's repetitious, circular, predictable communication patterns reveal the balance. . . . When the family's homeostasis is precarious, members exert much effort to maintain it."[6] John and Mary have "understood" each other's intentions well enough and have responded in kind to each other so that they feel they will gain some satisfactions of needs within the marriage and are now willing to commit themselves to each other.

Marital Contract

The marriage license is society's recognition of the desire and willingness of the couple to live together in marriage. The marital contract, both overt and covert, is the basis of the couple's common life. Clifford Sager has developed his understanding of marital systems around the idea of the contract. He says:

The marital system comes into existence under the following conditions: when each individual makes an investment in the system consonant with his or her willingness and ability to give and receive; when the goals and purposes of the new system (marriage) are more or less defined on various levels of awareness and may be constantly reexamined and reaffirmed as changed; when roles, tasks, responsibilities and functions for each person are assigned or assumed in order to achieve the new goals and purposes; and when some method of communication is developed so that intelligence can be transmitted.[7]

Sager believes that the woman and man both bring their individual contracts to the marriage. These contracts are based on expectations of marriage (e.g., for a loyal mate, for support against the rest of the world, for a relationship until death do us part); upon biological and psychological needs (e.g., independence-dependence, activity-passivity, close-ness-distance); and upon problem areas (e.g., communication, intellectual differences, energy levels). In order for there to be an *interactive* contract the couple must put their individual contracts on the table, discuss them, modify them according to the spouse's responses, and react in an open and collaborative way to the spouse's individual contract. The interactive contract should be worked out before marriage, ideally in premarital counseling.[8] If it is not, such a working out of an interactive contract will be a necessary part of the settling down process of the first year of marriage. Sager concludes:

The interactive contract provides the operational field in which each struggles with the other to achieve fulfillment of his own individual contract, including all the realistic, unrealistic and ambivalent clauses that it contains. It is the place where each partner tries to achieve his own objectives and force the other to behave in accordance with his design of the marriage.[9]

Mary Jo Bane believes that couples should be required to submit contracts, even though simply worked out as to area of responsibilities regarding work, child support, housing, in order to obtain a license to marry. Society currently exacts more from teen-agers to get a driver's license than it does from adults to qualify for marriage. Surely the clergy, as agents of the community, could take this step in their premarital counseling, working with couples in making their individual contracts an interactive contract before they take the step of marriage.

2. Family Development

When couples contract a marriage, they believe that the "loved one" incarnates all they have ever desired in a mate and hope things will never change. In a matter of months of living together each will be disillusioned by the other, and they will discover that *change* is the name of the game. Clifford Sager says: "Contracts on any and all levels are dynamic and may change at any point in the marital relationship. . . . Such changes frequently take place when there is a significant modification of needs, expectations, or role demands of one or both partners, or when a new force enters the marital system."[10]

The final axiom states: The marriage and family system changes as members grow, life situations alter, and the couple/family cycles through phases of development necessitating new understandings of roles and new working out of contracts. During the rest of the chapter we want to examine the family life cycle, looking at the developmental tasks at each stage and the changes of contract and role behavior necessary for each family member to negotiate each stage.

Evelyn Millis Duvall developed a family cycle, using traditional sex roles and phased to the birth and growth of children within the home.[11] We want to modify the family cycle somewhat, taking account of the rethinking of sex roles, and the recent longitudinal research of both adult men and women—in particular as related to marriage and the family. The research of George Vaillant at Harvard on the "ninety-five men of the classes of 1942, '43, and '44 of Harvard College" and that of Daniel Levinson at Yale of the adult development of a selected population of 40 men add new insight to what happens today in early and mid-marriage. One must allow for the fact that the sexual revolution and its impact on the family will continue into the rest of the century. Nevertheless, it is important to formulate the course of marriage and family development again, while recognizing that the shape of marriage and family life of the future is not yet clear.

A. Early Marriage

Sidney Jourard recently wrote a provocative essay entitled, "Marriage is for Life." He was not talking about

A Family Life Cycle

	1	2	3	4	5	6	7	8

Family Developmental tasks of each stage

1. Marriage to first birth
   – Moving from individual to couple role
   – Disillusionment of engagement period to realistic appraisal of mate

2. Birth to entry of first child in school
   – Moving from couple to parent roles
   – Nurturing, being responsible for child
   – Responding to child's needs and interests so as to promote growth and learning

3. Elementary school age
   – Launching child into educational community
   – Maintaining responsible ties to child

4. Adolescent age
   – Establishing balance between emotional distance and support as child enters puberty
   – Developing outside interests beyond family

5. Launching period
   – Letting youth go to begin college or work experience and leave home
   – Supporting young adults in not quite responsible period

6. Empty nest period
   – Reestablishing the marital relationship; planning for retirement
   – Extending family, so that children feel connected to your generation

7. Death of spouse and widowhood
   – Experiencing the grief process
   – Adapting to single living or remarriage

lifetime marriage, but saying that "marriage is to enhance life . . . it is not so much an answer as it is a search."[12] He used his own marriage as an example. He and his wife had been married seven years when they separated. He had been unfaithful and, when confronted with her knowledge of the fact, he left her. They decided to remarry a month later, and to work on their marriage. Each began to accept the other person as he or she truly was, and to be open about what they wanted to receive as well as what each could give to the other in terms of love, dialogue, and mutual support. At each stage of their marriage over nearly twenty-five years, they had to take account of the changes in the other and in their life situation and make new contracts. He concluded: "I do not know how many marriages I have had now, but I am married to a different woman of the same name in ways that are suited to our present stage of growth as human beings."[13]

Marriage contracts are worked out differently depending upon the ages of the spouses and upon the nature of their premarital contract. The sexual revolution is making a difference in both factors, in particular in the conjugal living relationships among some young couples, meaning that they decide for marriage after a period of time in which they have lived together as lovers.

Let's look in more detail at the age of marriage. Some youth marry in their teens, either foregoing further education and launching into the world of work immediately after high school, or attempting to combine their education with marriage. Youthful marriage is precarious at best: the young man and woman are not out of adolescence and are still struggling with their identity, with vocational choices to make, and often experience difficulty separating themselves from the parental nest. (See Launch Period.) The highest incidence of divorce occurs at this period. Daniel Levinson calls this period the Early Adult transition and says,

If a man married during his Early Adult transition, as about half of our sample did, he has had little experience in forming peer relationships with adult women. For him, courtship and marital choice are likely to be bound up with . . . Early Adult transition, and especially with efforts to separate from his parents. He wants very much to be very grown up and, at the same time, to maintain his pre-adult ties to parents and others. He is hardly a step beyond adolescence when sex is often a frightening mystery or an exploitative act.[14]

In 1974 the average age for marriage was twenty-three for men and twenty-one for women, and 42 percent of all twenty-year-old women were married. Those who marry at this stage are just beginning to enter the adult world.[15] Levinson says the men, both professional and working class, could be called "novices," learning a trade and getting established in a job. Gail Sheehy concluded from her interviewing women that they mature at a different rate from men and may enter marriage in their twenties prematurely before they have a chance to get established in the work world. These women who form a "complete me" or coattail marriage do not understand that they have been sold short and do not become restive in their marriages until they are approaching thirty. The conflict between getting married and having a career is only felt keenly by college-trained women today, and this phenomenon did not become apparent until the 1970s. Postponing marriage, therefore, is a middle-class, educated thing to do among women in their twenties.

Men, on the other hand, desire marriage as much as women do. If they have postponed marriage, either because of fear of a long-term commitment or because they have been preoccupied with getting established in their job or career, they begin to look seriously in their late twenties for a mate. Levinson says,

During this age 30 transition . . . being married is usually experienced as a gap in his life or a problem. The man who begins married life during this period, as 20% of our sample did, possibly knows more about himself and his relationships with women, and may have resolved more fully some of the conflicts from the past. But he also may be marrying under pressure; this may be his last chance. He may decide to marry in an effort to normalize his life more than for love.[16]

The other fact we want to examine is the conjugal couple who decide to marry. Although common-law marriages have been recognized as a lower-class phenomenon, and upper-class couples have taken mistresses in several cultures in North America, the practice of young adults' living together openly has not become a trend until this decade. Beginning around university campuses in the late 1960s, the practice has spread to the large cities and now can be observed even in small towns in mid-America. In a class of twenty-five students which I taught in California in 1971, I asked the students to report a verbatim premarital counseling interview in which they were then engaged in the churches where they worked. Not a single instance was reported in which the couple was not living together before they came to be married!

Certain characteristics are evident in the conjugal couple which comes to be married: (1) They go through the settling down process and preliminary contracting while living together. (2) One member—usually the man—has desired an "escape hatch" out of the arrangement if it does not appear to work out. (3) The couple are often ruthlessly honest with each other regarding their needs and confront each other openly regarding their deficiencies. (4) The missing element of commitment—"to love and to cherish in sickness and in health, poverty and in wealth, till death do us part"—in the marriage vows is needed to bring stability to the relationship and recognition by the community. Such a couple will need premarital counseling of the contracting sort in order to stabilize the relationship. My practice is to see all couples six months after marriage to review the contract so that the settling down process may be completed.

With less clearly defined marital roles, and with a wife in particular whose consciousness has been raised and who wants to be equal to her partner in the relationship, the period of early marriage is very important. The husband and wife will need to attend to their development tasks and intentionally to contract: whether both will work and where, whose career to follow if both have careers, whether or not to have children and, if so, how many (many couples will decide not to have children or, if so, to have only one), and what life-style to follow. Many couples today will choose a simple life-style, choosing some form of cooperative living, some way of actively showing concern for the poor and the economically exploited, limiting their financial spending to human projects rather than simply spending for more and more luxuries. If they live in an area where poverty and exploitation are visible, it is difficult to understand how couples of conscience can choose differently.

B. *Early Marriage with a Child*

Gail Sheehy has given us three categories by which we can understand early marriage and the family, each of which has different developmental tasks. I want to spell these out now and then to illustrate them with case vignettes from three families. They include the nuturing mother who defers achievement; the achieving wife who defers nurturance; and the integrating couple.[17]

1. *The Nurturing Mother Who Defers Achievement*

The developmental tasks of young parents is to shift from couple roles to parent roles. When a couple begins a family immediately—whether the child is planned or unplanned—they must reorganize their family and talk through their responsibilities respecting the care and nurture of the child.

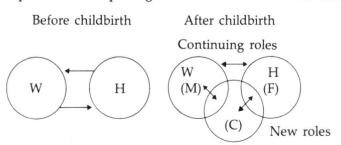

Before childbirth   After childbirth

Continuing roles

W   H   W (M)   H (F)

(C)   New roles

The mother may choose to leave her job and to devote herself full-time to the care of the baby. If so, the couple follows a traditional way of assigning parent roles: mother equals care-giver, father equals breadwinner. The father may help with the care of the baby when he is home, but it is agreed that the primary responsibility for the feeding and nurturing of the child is assumed by the mother.

If the woman defers returning to her job and if the couple decides that she should devote herself exclusively to family care-giving until the children are school age, they should realize that the woman is making a personal sacrifice. When she returns to work she probably will begin at the bottom of the pay scale. She may find it necessary to return to school at that time in order to bring her skills back or up to date. And by that time (age thirty plus) she may want to change fields and to prepare herself for a career which allows for the expression of her total self. Rearing a young family is immensely rewarding. But it can also deplete energy levels and lower self-esteem. Many women who have devoted themselves exclusively to child rearing for ten years may feel incapable of entering the job market again.

Marital satisfaction drops sharply with the coming of the first baby.[18] The couple will need to adapt to each other's sexual needs during pregnancy and immediately afterward. Time to be together and to go out together must be found. Otherwise, the couple may find the baby driving a wedge between them. These problems we shall discuss further in the chapter on *family crises*. Suffice it to say now that the first major recontracting in the marriage occurs with the coming of the first child.

Vignette

Betty and Len are a modern couple in many respects. They met in a city university during the early seventies. Len was a student activist and demonstrated against the Vietnam war. One would not have expected him to settle down early, but would have thought that he would work for a while as a roustabout on a tramp steamer or a cowboy on a Western ranch. Until he met Betty he appeared to be unsettled. She had been very popular with men, had worked as a salesperson at several department stores, and spent a year as a community volunteer with a social agency. She did not prepare herself for a particular vocation but vacillated between art and politics. Len proposed one week, and they were married the next. They settled down to marriage like old hands and had their first child, a girl, eighteen months later.

Betty is by temperament a care-giver, and the bulk of the child care fell to her. Len spent his extra time working overtime at his job and at night school studying for a master's degree in social work. They made a down payment on a house, and Len fixed up the spare room for the little girl, using his carpentry skills. Betty and Len have not yet decided about having more children. They appear to be happy in the contracting which they have done concerning their almost exclusive taking of the child-rearing and breadwinning roles. Betty has a part-time position, since their daughter is a year old, teaching parent education classes at a community school. They employ babysitters and find time for vacations together. Whether Betty returns to full-time work again is an open question.

2. *Achievers Who Defer Nurturing*

The woman who marries today and delays having a child so that she may follow her career discovers about age thirty that she had better begin her family or physiologically she may lose the opportunity. (Medicine has shown that babies conceived just before menopause run the risk of mental retardation and other infirmities.) Many young adults concerned about overpopulation become conscious of what having a child of their own would mean: transforming them from a simple dyad to a family. The urge to nurture is as strong in some men as it is in their wives.

Recontracting may be more difficult for the deferring family than for the couple who have their children earlier. The woman has established her identity around her work, and she does not want to sacrifice it upon the altar of child care. Maternity leaves may be taken—in fact, the new mother may consider taking an extended leave of six months or more during the nursing period. The new father may want to become more involved in child care than his traditional breadwinner father. Becoming part of Lamaze class in childbirth, being present and a support to his wife during childbearing, and entering more completely into nurturing, he may find fatherhood as engaging as his job. Suffice it to say that couples who defer having children should enter a crucial period of recontracting when the child finally arrives on the scene.

Vignette

Bill and Sally are a little old to be having babies. They were married fifteen years ago while in college and postponed having children while Bill was in the Navy and she took up her career in order to finance Bill in graduate school.

Bill took a position with a family-owned company and worked his way up to a middle management position. Sally continued in a career in nursing and, at thirty-five, is now a teacher of nurses in a university program. They have been able to accumulate all they want so far as savings, a home and furnishings. They attempted an adoption five years ago and after nearly a year's work it came to naught. Both are religious and active in their church, a Quaker meeting. They had fairly well accepted that it was God's will that they not have children.

Then last spring Sally missed several periods, and she was sure she was pregnant. About the same time they received notification that a baby was due for adoption next Christmas and since their adoption forms were in order they could be first on the list to receive the child. They were in a quandary at first: should they give up their adoption plans? If Sally were not pregnant, then they might not get a child since they were getting too old to be considered. They decided to go ahead with the adoption proceedings. Summer found Sally definitely pregnant and the baby due at Christmas.

They felt God's hand was in the events. They had cared for twin boys once earlier when their parents were away and thought they could handle twins this time. They sought out a house with adequate facilities and moved in early in December. Their daughter, Anne, was born by the Lamaze method, with Bill's participation. Their adopted child, Alma, was brought to them a week later. Sally decided to nurse them both.

She obtained maternity leave through the month of January. She said the only difficulty was in getting the school where she works to allow her to find a nursing room for the children. The dean was reluctant to do this as he believed it would establish a precedent. Bill took a week's vacation in December to help Sally, and they then obtained the services of a grandmother five days a week while Sally was teaching.

Both want to continue their careers. It would be difficult for Sally to give hers up at this point when she is so far advanced. Bill finds it difficult to be home other than on weekends since he is in a job that requires more than forty hours a week. The little babies have adjusted to their schedule and are doing nicely. The parents, a little haggard with the pace of keeping two babies, feel that it is well worth the extra trouble. However, they believe that their jobs are what do not bend much to make room for parenthood at their ages.

3. *Integrators*

Gail Sheehy is of the opinion that the integrator is a new breed of couple in the United States. They are the men and women who try to combine work and family so that they share equally in both. The house-husband and the father-nurturer are role reversals, probably too counter-cultural for most career-oriented and/or traditional males in North America. Paul Graubard's fifteen-month experiment in which he took complete charge of the house and family of four while his wife was sole breadwinner taught the professor much practical child psychology, but moved the couple to decide to become integrators.[19]

Integration involves role sharing both the roles of breadwinner and parent-child nurturer. With more women in the work market (now more than half are working during the child-bearing years) the man cannot hide in his work at part-time jobs in order to allow time for parenthood. Vocations such as teaching, various kinds of creative arts, professions such as ministry, law or counseling—anything which is not bound to a rigid time schedule may be opted for. At least it means arranging for the wife to continue her outside work life as soon as the initial childbearing and nurturing is complete. And it allows the husband to invest himself as fully in parenthood as his wife does, actively participating in the early care-giving of the infant and becoming a teacher-companion when the child begins to mature.

Vignette

Lon and Bobbie were married in college, but each was headed for a career, so they delayed having children. They spent several years out of college living abroad in Germany and, when they returned from Europe, immediately enrolled in separate graduate programs in international relations and social work. Only at thirty-five and thirty-two, when they were finally settled in an Eastern city, did they feel that the time was right for children. Bobbie took leave from her agency, and Lon pitched in to help run the house when the baby, a boy they called Tommy, arrived.

Both Lon and Bobbie wanted to continue working where they were, and Lon did not want to see Bobbie give up her good position; so from the beginning they tried to integrate work and family. They spent time matching their schedules, Bobbie working weekends and evenings and Lon covering those periods when his teaching at the university allowed him to be off. They bought a house in an area of the city where other young parents were attempting an integrated life-style. Five of these families got together and worked out an arrangement whereby one parent was home each afternoon to look after the children of the five families. Tommy was entered in a day school at age three, and now at six is in a Montessori school near his home. Evenings and weekends Lon and Bobbie give Tommy their first attention and spend time at the zoo or children's museum or the circus.

This family does not plan to have other children. They have talked it over and have several reasons: their ages; their priority they give to their work; and their responsibilities in the community and the church. In addition, they are both sensitive to the need to limit population growth. Tommy does not appear to have suffered from his parents' life-style; in fact, he is a bright though quiet child at six. He has playmates from the groups with which he stays in the afternoon and will miss them next year when his parents plan a sabbatical in another country.

Lon and Bobbie speak of the ideal arrangement where each would work three-fourths of the time and be able to give more time to the family, the community, and the church. Lon has taken steps toward implementing this arrangement, and Bobbie has plans to do so in the near future.

C. *Parents of Adolescents*

The first major change parents experience with the family is when the child starts to school. I shall not devote time here to this period or to the discipline problems of childhood. The chapter on *family crises* will focus on some of these problems. The onset of puberty—from ages twelve to fifteen with today's well-nourished middle-class children (earlier or later with some from poorer backgrounds)—projects a new situation on the family and requires the parents to recontract with each other and with the youth.

What are the developmental tasks of parents of adolescents? They are keyed first to the changes which the youth is going through and, second, to the change which the parent-couple are experiencing in the marriage relationship. Therefore, the parents need (1) to recognize the emotional shifts which the youth is experiencing centering in sexual feelings, a growing body, the struggle with his/her identity, the need for peer approval, and the need to control his or her own life; (2) to relate to the youth not as a child but as an "emerging adult"; (3) to establish a flexible balance between distance (the teen-ager's need to be alone at times) and support (the youth's need to depend upon his parents as he did as a child); and (4) to relate to each other as marriage partners at mid-life with the changes brought on by aging and shifting work and play needs.

Parents of youth are often unprepared for the normal developmental crises which youth experience at the onset of puberty. It is a quiet change, marked by the first menstruation of the girl and the first seminal emission of the boy.[20] These pubertal changes signal for the parents the whole range of emotional changes the youth will go through. He or she is capable of reproducing, and this change pushes the young man or woman toward adulthood over the next decade or so. Parents and youth need to stay in conversation through this period although at a different level and with different outcomes than at childhood. It is not a dominant–submissive posture as it was probably just a year earlier, but now approaches conversation between equals, with the parents giving the youth more and more responsibility for themselves.

The identity struggle which Erikson puts as the key to understanding adolescence involves parents as much as it does youth. J. E. Marcia, of the University of British Columbia, studied youth and their parents and discovered four ways in which the identity crisis was resolved during adolescence. He called them the moratorium way, the identity-foreclosed way, the identity-diffused way, and the identity-achieved way.[21] Each youth works out his identity crisis differently depending upon his parents' way of relating to him through the teen years. Some youth find the identity struggle too difficult and put the questions of who they are and what they want "on ice" until their twenties. Their parents probably continue to relate to them as children, keeping them dependent and exercising control over their choices of friends, colleges, jobs, and such. The identity-foreclosed group also have difficulty finding emotional distance from parents and may make choices but ones which reflect the values and identity of the parents. The son may choose to study law at the same school in which his father studied law; the daughter may marry right out of high school as her mother did. The identity-diffused group do not rebel against their parents but many become inwardly alienated from them while obeying them outwardly. They find themselves dependent on their parents but powerless in their teens and vaguely unhappy on going to college or plugging into the value systems their parents represent. But they may not awaken to their unhappiness until some time in their twenties. The identity-achieved group use adolescence for developing independence from parents and for actualizing their budding powers—whether in academics, sports, or heterosexual relations. Parents of such youth find a way of balancing emotional distance and support and rejoice in the growth of their young people.

The parents themselves will face changes in their mid-thirties and forties which reflect their changing relationship to each other as well as their children. The mid-life crisis may be experienced differently by men than by women. Gail Sheehy's thesis in *Passages* is that men and women are out of synchronization in mid-life.

During the twenties when a man gains confidence by leaps and bounds, a married woman is usually losing the superior assurance she once had as an adolescent. When a man passes 30 and wants to settle down, a woman is often becoming restless. And just at that point around 40, when a man feels himself to be standing on a precipice, his strength, power, dreams and illusions slipping away beneath him, his wife is likely to be brimming with ambition to climb her own mountain.[22]

Depending on the kind of contract the couple has worked out regarding parenting and their life of work, they will need now to recontract, taking account of several changes in their life: (1) their changing relationship to adolescent children; (2) their own changing needs for intimacy, distance, companionship, and a separate life which allows room for each to grow; (3) the family's total needs, including savings for college or getting young people started in business or in marriage, the changing housing needs, and the need perhaps to move to a different community to allow for the couple's careers; (4) the couple's career plans, which need to take account of the wife as fully as the husband as she begins to develop competencies and desires to push her career as vigorously as did her husband in the earlier period. A film like Ingmar Bergman's *Scenes from a Marriage* is based on the experience of a "happily married couple" each of whom failed in mid life to take account of the changes which mid-life brought to the other, and their "total communication" made them fully conscious of how she had grown beyond him and now wanted her freedom.

Vignette

Bob, forty-six, a lawyer, and Mary, forty-four, a home economist, have four teen-agers. They were married just out of college, and Mary did not work outside the home until the past year, when the cost of college loomed ahead of them. She has "majored in family" and done a great deal of volunteer work within the community. Both she and Bob are social activists but have carved out a large place for the family, particularly enjoying summer vacations camping together.

Their children are all activists, with Sam, eighteen, setting the sights for all the rest. He has been very good at school, and particularly in music. He so far outdistanced Dave, sixteen, the second son, that Dave chose not to compete in scholastics but majored in sports, becoming an excellent basketball player. Peter, the third son, at fifteen is also not interested in school but likes mechanics of any sort, spending much of his free time fixing up old automobiles. Judy, thirteen, is just entering the teen years and is quiet and retiring, except that at times when shopping with her mother, she opens up.

The family moved from the suburbs to the city six years ago and, with more blacks in the schools than they were accustomed to, Dave was the one who took the knocks, getting into a number of scuffles until he made his way with new friends. Judy is now having trouble sorting out the gang she wants to run with, having found her new crowd rather fast and involved in shoplifting, so that she dropped out and went back to old friends. Both Sam and Dave have steady girl friends and are on their own since they drive. Their parents do not hold them to specific times to get in, but Pete and Judy do have curfews. All the children have jobs and earn money of their own to spend as they see fit.

The Browns are a church couple and have had difficulty getting their older children to continue to attend church, particularly, they say, when the youth go through an "atheist" period. Grace at meals continues to be said even through this time, and there is the expectation that the children will go to church at least once on Sunday. They feel that their values are communicated directly and indirectly at mealtimes and during one-to-one conversations. Although neither Bob nor Mary has engaged in formal sex education with them, they have talked with the boys as *Playboy* magazines are brought into the home, and feel this phase has passed now that the boys are going with "real" girls.

Expectations are that the children will finish college, and, although Dave has previously talked of doing something else, he now sees the advantage of going on to school and preparing to become a physical education teacher or doing something connected with sports. Pete talks of becoming a farmer, and Judy wants nothing more than to get married and have children. It is Sam who carries the family's highest expectations into a musical career.

Flexibility is a part of this family as they have learned to treat each teen-ager differently, honoring his talents and specific needs. Yet the values of human rights, justice, and fair play have been taught both directly and indirectly. Although the teen-agers have not tested these values away from home, the Browns feel they are about ready to let them go try their wings.

D. *Parents at the Launch*

When youths leave home for work, for the armed service, or for college, parents launch them out of the nest and must recognize that their major parental responsibilities are over. The developmental tasks of this stage involve letting go of the youth emotionally while still supporting them economically and offering whatever guidance is asked for. The meta-adult period is one in which young people are not quite adult. At sixteen they can drive; at eighteen, vote, serve in the armed forces, and in most states buy beer at a liquor store. However, they come back home periodically—for a summer during college, for a year or two in their twenties as they get started in a job or complete graduate school. Some young adults in some areas may live with or near their parents while attending a community college or start an early marriage—all of which means that many young people in their early twenties may earnestly desire emotional independence, but they are not completely financially responsible.

Parents at this stage need to face their own developmental tasks. Primary is getting acquainted again as wife and husband who now have fewer people under the roof and much more time to be together. Menopause has to be faced by the woman, and the loss of energy by both makes it necessary to live at a slower pace. Nevertheless, adequate exercise and a responsible diet make mid-life not an unpleasant experience but one which allows both man and woman to age with dignity and beauty. The letting go of children is experienced by the couple as grief. When they lose their own parents at this stage they may grieve, and the loss of children compounds the feeling of sorrow. Some women who go through the change of life, even though not working through a loss, may get depressed.

Careers of both husband and wife may need to be talked through as they decide whose career to follow and what accommodations each will need to make in "cutting back" or changing location or even changing careers. The combination of high commitment to work, heavy financial pressure, and community responsibility may take marriage partners away from each other at a time when they need to recontract and talk through ways they want to chart the rest of their lives before retirement. Reevaluating priorities in their marriage and family, their community responsibilities, and their life values may take more than just an evening talk; it may require a longer period when they do some soul searching together. Weekend church retreats, marriage enrichment events, and family clusters are important at this period in order for couples to find the support necessary for them to do the contracting they need to do together. (See p. 174 on family clusters.)

Vignette

Rob and Nellie have been married for twenty-eight years and have two sons, ages twenty-six and twenty-four. They are both college educated, Rob having gone on to earn a master's degree in public health and now occupying a responsible position as the head of a social agency. Nellie is artistic and has worked as a manager of an art store; she is now working at planning a house for their later years.

Rob and Nellie thought they had launched their sons two years ago, when John, the first son, was married and took his first position with a large company, and George completed his college education and began teaching in a junior high school. They sold their large home and temporarily moved in with Nellie's sister until they could find a smaller house.

They both report not a sense of loss but a sense of relief in the launch of their sons. John had not demanded much from them, always having been one to seek his own counsel; and as soon as he was married, he appeared content to start his own home. He and his wife had their first child last spring. George, however, was always close to his parents and has wanted to be in the middle of everything that happened in the home. He suffered an accident in junior high and needed special attention, and this, too, brought him closer to his parents, particularly his mother. Both Bob and Nellie felt that teaching would make George more independent.

They found an apartment with only one bedroom while they were planning their home for retirement. A crisis occurred when George decided to go on to graduate school and moved back home. He took over the living room for his own and became very much a part of the family again. What appeared to be a launch now became a return to the roost for George and an adjustment on Rob and Nellie's part. The releasing of the second son was not accomplished and it is likely that the launch, when it occurs, will be more of a crisis than they had at first thought.

One would have to conclude that the families represented in this chapter are in transition. Some recognize the change in their family homeostasis better than others. However, the reader must readily perceive that today's families need added flexibility as well as the support of each member in order to manage these changes. From here we shall move to consider family crisis periods of intense challenge to the structure as well as the functioning of healthy families.

Exercises

(1) Visit a day nursery, an elementary school, a middle school or a high school. Make arrangements to visit several classes. If you go to a high school, talk with the

counseling department about the developmental tasks of adolescents.

(2) Arrange to view the film *Saturday Morning* with parents of adolescents. Have your minister, a high school teacher, or a counselor talk to you following the film concerning the developmental concerns of youth.

(3) Arrange a weekend retreat with parents of junior highs or senior highs to talk over the parenting responsibilities of youth of this age. Have the young people come on Sunday to lead the worship service and to spend the rest of the retreat with their parents to dialogue with them concerning follow-through at home.

(4) Discuss the contracting or recontracting which was necessary for the couple in each vignette at the particular developmental phase of their marriage.

Chapter IV
Family Crises

Every one then who hears these words of mine and does them will be like a wise man who built his house upon the rock; and the rain fell, and the floods came, and the winds blew and beat upon that house, but it did not fall, because it had been founded on the rock. And everyone who hears these words of mine and does not do them will be like a foolish man who built his house upon the sand; and the rain fell, and the floods came, and the winds blew and beat against that house, and it fell; and great was the fall of it.
Matt. 7:24-27 RSV

Nothing tests a family network so much as a disruption of its ordinary way of doing things. Without much planning, activity within a family falls into a routine and expected way of meeting one another's needs. This habitual way of acting and interacting must change when a family member gets sick, changes jobs, has a baby, leaves for college, or dies. The other family members are thrown into a crisis and soon realize they must shift family responsibilities and learn to cope in different ways.

This happened to our family recently when my father-in-law became sick. He lived alone and needed nursing care and help in getting his meals. My wife, being an only child, was the one who had to go to take care of him. In the meantime, I had been scheduled for surgery in the hospital and, although it was not a major operation, we realized I would go into surgery without her being present. She returned from the care of her father the day after surgery and was able to visit me then in the hospital. However, she indicated that she felt pulled in two directions by the double crisis. And I was much relieved to see her, to know of her father's improvement, and to have her near during my convalescence.

1. The Nature of Crisis

Gerald Caplan defines a crisis as an "upset in the steady state of an individual or a family."[1] An individual experiences a crisis when he becomes sick. The body's physiological system is out of balance. There is a need for bed rest, change of diet, surgical repair, and a diminished schedule. But as illustrated above, every individual crisis can be looked at from within a family system as well. My father-in-law's illness coming at the same time as my surgery put stress upon our family system and was felt particularly by my wife. Had she had siblings they could have been called to help her father at the time I was to be hospitalized. But, because there are none, she felt she must go to her father in order to get things stabilized and then return to be with me during my surgery. It should be noted that our family system includes her father even though he is of another generation and lives in another place.

In a family a crisis may be of two kinds: either immediate and situational, or developmental and longitudinal. A situational crisis is one in which there is a sudden change in typical patterns of family behavior caused by a loss of basic supplies and the meeting of individual needs. The father loses his job and must accept a position in another city. This necessitates the family's selling their home and moving; the mother giving up her part-time job, son and daughter leaving their school and friends, and the whole family uprooting from their church and community connections. Situations which upset the family system and put stress upon individual members are: illness; moving; sudden loss of home through fire, flood, or other disaster; the arrest of a family member; bringing a new member into the family; death; and divorce.

Developmental and longitudinal crises are of the sort described by Erik Erikson and which we examined in the last chapter from the standpoint of the family—namely, the birth of a child; his starting to school; his adolescence; his leaving home for work or college; his marriage; and the retirement of one or both from work. This kind of crisis comes at certain transition points in the development of the individual from birth to death. It can usually be anticipated and planned for by the family. It requires a change in the way in which the family fulfills certain roles within the home and copes with the demands of the community.

The community in which the family lives may help precipitate a crisis and/or show a certain tolerance for family breakdown. Much controversy, particularly in black groups, has been generated over Daniel Moynihan's appraisal of the black family as unstable and matriarchal. Are the statistics slanted toward judging black families by white family standards? David Lynn, however, sees "family" as having a different status in the black community. Marriage is looked on as a private relationship and one which concerns only the couple and does not have to meet community expectations so much as white marriage does. He cites studies by Virginia Young and concludes:

The black family maintains strong ties over three or four generations. These multigenerational ties lend stability to the system by protecting unwed mothers, who may have a series of unions. The black man, however, has a role in the system. . . . His absence from the household of his own children and his periodic moves to different households at least while he is young, are an expression of a value system that prizes true and compatible relationships between men and women.[2]

Living in the inner city where drug trafficking, prostitution, and shoplifting are established patterns among adolescents affects the family structure and relationships. Similarly, living in rural areas where isolation from other youth, attending consolidated schools which require several hours' commuting by bus, and necessary work on a family farm also affects family structure and relationships. The milieu in which the family resides has a direct bearing on how families view themselves and what they consider a crisis as well as how they go about dealing with the circumstances of their lives.

Gerald Caplan has helped us to understand that a crisis has a natural history and can be understood to go through various phases. Depending on the workability of previous problem-solving techniques or the willingness of family members to go along with assigned systemic roles, things may not go beyond phase 1. If the family is continuously stressed by outside forces (environmental—storms, floods, accidents, etc.), the crisis accelerates and pushes the family into phase 2. If extra-family events produce added stress and intramural family coping procedures are not working, the family descends to phase 3. Phase 4 is "copelessness"—the stage we shall look at time and again in the counseling chapters, when the family members are stuck and nothing seems to be helping them out of their mounting troubles. Caplan's widely used four-phase cycle of individual and family crisis is as follows:

Phase 1: The individual or family under increasing tension seeks to solve the problem in former ways that have worked.

Phase 2: Tension increases as the old methods fail to bring relief or the problems do not succeed in getting solved.

Phase 3: The individual or family mobilizes emergency problem-solving methods under mounting tension and seeks to redefine the problem, relate the problem to a different area of experience, and resolve the difficulty.

Phase 4: If the individual or family cannot then resolve the problem, the tension and stress may mount beyond the limit of tolerance. If the individual or family cannot obtain relief at this crucial point, they may undergo lasting disruption and eventually death of the individual or disintegration of the family.[3]

Jesus' designation of houses built on sand or on rock is a carpenter's way of recognizing that some families have more tolerance for crisis than others. The care and attention which family members give to the foundation of their life together will be demonstrated at the time of storm by its ability to meet the crisis. In systems language some families are open systems; i.e., they provide for change, offer choices, and depend on successfully meeting reality for their continuing life. Some families are closed systems which provide little change, depend on edict and law and order, and operate through force, both physical and psychological.[4] Both situational and developmental crises give a family a chance to break out of habitual patterns of interacting. They provide a family with the opportunities for growth and development, on the one hand; or, on the other hand, the crisis challenges the family and can precipitate its dissolution and destruction if the challenge is not met. Whether the family engages in counseling or not, they need to become aware of their characteristic ways of meeting crisis and what their resources are, both psychological and spiritual. Such assessment can be made at a church family retreat or as a part of a family cluster group.[5] Situational and developmental crises will confront the family as surely as the seasonal rains fall. How families manage their crises will depend upon each individual member's level of spiritual growth and maturity and the strength of family bonds which each member has developed. Hearing God's Word and heeding it for a family implies family worship, but it also demands open communication between family members and each strengthening the other in fair weather and in foul.

2. Family Analysis

Medicine and, in particular, psychiatry have moved in the direction of the prevention of illness. Gerald Caplan and others point to the devastating and destructive influence of racial prejudice, poor housing, inadequate diet, and poor community structure. The building of strong family systems is seen as one way among others of preventing emotional illness and breakdown under particular stress.[6] Now we want to investigate the ways families can look at themselves, either with or without a family counselor, in order to test their strength and their vulnerability to stress. A family may well analyze their weaknesses and strengths in good times so that they may be aware of how they will fare when the rains, floods, and winds beat upon their house. Some of the best analyses of problems are done in calm, say family therapists, or at least when most family members are able to work at their situation.

In assessing the cohesiveness of a family—their internal resilience—one first should look at the strengths and weaknesses of individual family members. What are the coping devices of mother and father? Of each individual child? How have they handled previous situational crises, such as an illness or a move? How have they handled previous "passages," such as the child's move from nursery school to kindergarten? How have the parents handled the launch of their children to college? The answers to these questions give some idea of how much the parents have individuated—i.e., developed what Murray Bowen calls "solid self"—and are no longer operating out of "pseudo self" or living according to the script presented to them by their parents or grandparents. They also indicate how well their children are developing individual and healthy identities. On the positive side, they are neither so fused with parents that they depend upon them for their emotional supplies nor so cut off from them that they are left without a support in the community and a family tradition upon which to depend. The older generation guides and helps socialize the younger generation as it grows, giving them enough "tether" to reach out toward persons outside the family—particularly after they start to school—but also being present when children need to fall back upon family support to regroup and to gather strength.

Let me give an example of an adolescent whom I studied fifteen years ago as a part of a longitudinal study. Helen was rated by psychologists as highly vulnerable to stress in infancy, childhood, and early adolescence. She had health problems in childhood, was lonely and isolated at age eight by a move her parents made, and felt herself less accepted by her mother than her older sister. When I saw her at early adolescence she was learning to use her religious faith as a way of coping with stress, and was beginning to overcome her extreme vulnerability.

One of the psychologists summarizes:

What was not explicit was the slow sequence of her childhood experience, from illness to health, from feelings of deprivation to capability to meet her own needs, from naughty, brash demandingness to modulated and socially acceptable assertion, from being an odd-looking, vulnerable baby and sick child to becoming a lovely and healthy teenager. Her image also contained her ego ideal of the giving grandmother with whom she had evidently deeply identified, even while at puberty she increasingly identified with her own mother as well.[7]

The second area to investigate is the adequacy of supplies, both economic and emotional. For example, the crisis of sending children to college challenges the economic resources of the family. Perhaps the parents have saved money for this period, perhaps the youth has worked summers and after school and has funds for personal expenses. However, the cost of a college education puts a strain on the average family budget. The family needs to investigate borrowing on the father's insurance, having the mother take part-time work, or the youth may need to choose a community college and live at home rather than go to an expensive private school out of town. The emotional resources of a family are not quantitative. However, one can recognize that an emotionally repressed father who never has shown his feelings or provided emotional support for his family during ordinary times will be found grossly inadequate during a crisis. The child who has felt emotionally deprived throughout his development will feel little parental care and support when he goes through the crisis of puberty and gets into trouble at school. The inadequacy of emotional supplies is particularly evident in the case of Gary and Grandma in chapter 7.

Coping and management processes which family members develop in particular crises is a third focus of family analysis. Robert Beavers distinguishes between three types of family systems: (1) seriously disturbed or entropic; (2) mid-range or rigidly structured; and (3) healthy structure with flexibility.[8]

One may look at these three types of families in functional terms as well. One would then designate families as, first, the copeless, i.e., those who manage poorly in good times and for whom a crisis is simply too much. This family may totally disintegrate or one or another member may leave during a crisis. This family may live at the periphery of the community, like the Burk family reported in chapter 2. Second, there are the muddlers-through. These families are highly resistant to change and muddle through crises but at the expense of one or more family members. They are not efficient copers, but hold to outmoded coping devices through habit, tradition, or restricted outlook. Third, there are efficient copers. These families have sufficient problem-solving ability to develop new ways of coping through a crisis. It is this group one would hope to enlist within a community or church to be at the heart of family support programs.

The fourth area to examine is the faith commitment and practice of the family. Studies show that members of families with a religious orientation have a lower suicide rate than those who have no faith connection.[9] Such studies would appear to indicate that religion can help individuals develop coping devices to meet crises. Gordon Allport distinguished between intrinsic religion (held in and for itself) and extrinsic religion (held for ulterior purposes).[10] The intrinsic family practices its faith internally through prayer and meditation and externally through various ethical stances in the community, with no thought of reward, and holds its faith in good times as well as in bad. The extrinsic family uses its faith to find a magical solution to crises and goes to church to increase its business or status or reputation. Within the family itself extrinsic religion means following the rules and conforming to community mores out of fear or habit. A crisis pushes this family into a "rainy-day religion" and it returns to following the rules and conforming to community standards after the crisis is over.

Finally, one should look at the community resources upon which the family may draw during a crisis. These include the extended family, the church or other outside group to which the family belongs, and the larger community (town, state or nation). Let us look at the Chicano family as an example. The Chicano family is looked upon as one in which macho males lord it over submissive females and which therefore lacks internal strength. However, there is a popular Mexican joke that says: "If your wife asks you to jump out of the window, pray God that it's from the first floor." Evelyn P. Stevens sets the record straight about machismo in Latin America. She contends that machismo in males fits hand in glove with marianismo (from the veneration of Mary in Roman Catholic countries). The eternally adolescent, sexually active male, even when married, depends upon the powerless, virginal, and venerated female. She quotes Mexican psychiatrist Rogelio Diaz Guero, who says, "Far from being victims of this dichotomous portrayal of sex roles, Latin American women are the deliberate perpetrators of the myth. . . . In the Mexican family, for one reason or another, it appears that it was decided that the father should have the power and the mother should have the love (and the power of care)."[11] But such families fall back on the extended family to help in times of crisis. David Lynn reports also concerning Chicano families: "The traditional Mexican American family demands, but it also protects. Every individual is regarded as a walking symbol of his family. To bring shame on one's family is an unforgivable sin, but the family is also a sanctuary in a hostile world."[12]

There are churches, usually small in membership, which simulate an extended family and which rally behind a stricken member family. At the time of death they provide food and child care for the family and express their care and support into the months ahead. There are tightly knit communities in rural areas certainly, but also in inner cities and some cooperative developments in suburbs which rebuild homes of burned-out families, help those hit by flood or hurricane, and generally respond to the critical need of other families as if it were their own. The Salvation Army, Red Cross, police, and fire departments in major cities are trained to manage disasters and provide civic, state, and federal resources to people in crises. One has only to live through a crisis like the Johnstown flood of 1977 or the West Virginia industrial accident of 1978 to recognize the terrible impact of crises on families and the humanitarian response which they evoke. During a blackout, some people will surely loot; however, just as surely some ordinary persons will work for days without food or sleep to care for the helpless.

3. Major Indicators of Family Difficulty

The minister or family counselor should understand that certain behavior within the family indicates that members are not coping well with stress they are facing. Before proceeding on the premise that the family is in difficulty, however, the worker should understand that families operate in certain ways in good times and in bad. Knowing these elements of family life will enable the counselor to estimate a family crisis more accurately.

(a) Families develop "family rules" which are either implicit or explicit. These rules govern sequences of communication and behavior. A crisis interrupts and throws into disarray the rules by which a family has lived and necessitates their attempting to find the "rule book" again.

(b) Families develop a hierarchy, i.e., a structure by which power is allocated in order to accomplish certain tasks within the group. This hierarchy is generational between parents and young children; but it may be located in the father or the mother depending on competency and ability to maintain order and to get the job done. Again a crisis may throw the hierarchical structure of the family out of whack, and its members need to rethink the way matters have been arranged in the family.[13]

(c) In intimate relationships—mother/child; lover/beloved; husband/wife—fusion can occur, which means "the blurring of self boundaries."[14] One could say such persons had developed an *overdependency*, except that the relationship fluctuates and changes. During a crisis two overdependent persons may collapse like a house of cards and find that the strength to manage the crisis does not exist in either one. Or the crisis may bring out the strength in one and throw the other into a deeper dependency.

(d) Another tendency in families is to develop triangles. A two-party system is stable except during crisis. At that time, when anxiety increases, the more vulnerable person will involve a third person to alleviate the stress. An example is the overinvolved parent fused with the child who, when the child raises mayhem, calls the father to come from the study and settle the child down. Another example is the man who, displeased with his wife, gets involved in an extramarital affair.

(e) Families will *cut* themselves *off emotionally* from the immediately preceding generation in order to live their lives in the present. Thus the family member has unfinished business of an emotional nature to complete with his father, mother, sister, brother, or even grandfather. The individual will deny this connection and its importance by separation from the family home, running away, and trying to ignore family members. However, this kind of emotional cutoff in times of crisis will show itself as merely a denial of family connections and not an escape from them.

We shall deal more directly with family crises in the counseling sections; however, now let us merely indicate what some of the major indicators of family distress are so that the minister may be aware of them as he works with members of the parish. First, the husband and wife are involved in a marriage conflict. They are quarreling, and this information gives the pastor a clue that a crisis is either impending or in full swing. From a systems standpoint, the pastor is interested in the breakdown in communication between husband and wife and how this interrupts the family's equilibrium. Children will sense the parents' conflict even if the parents are not quarreling in front of them. Second, at least one of the spouses is not functioning adequately at work or in the home. This is expressed in physical or emotional illness, alcoholism, or altered behavior. The father may have lost his job and, after looking for work for a year's time, is not leaving the house at all but is merely sitting and brooding. All members are affected by the father's dysfunction. The mother must go out to work to earn enough to survive, and the children feel the emotional withdrawal of the father from the family circle. A third area is that of behavioral problems of one or several children. The failure of the children in school, their getting involved in shoplifting, drinking on school grounds, or sexual promiscuity all indicate some internal crisis within the family. Scapegoating—the projection of the family's troubles onto one child—may be indicated when one assesses the situation. However, when the parents bring the child to the church school teacher or the school counselor, or the child is brought to the parents for having cut school or broken the law, the crisis has broken out and the parents are then intensely involved. The cry for help—which the behavioral problem represents—now pushes the whole family into crisis and upsets the normal way of doing things at home.

During a crisis the family system suffers from an overloading of its circuits and finds that its characteristic ways of defending itself from outer stress and inner stress and inner anxiety are not working. The individual family members, held together in bonding and contracts, meeting one another's spoken and hidden agendas, cannot do business as usual—the crisis prevents that. However, the family system is resilient and bends and creaks and groans—much like the house caught in the rains and floods and winds. Whether it survives or falls depends on whether it is capable of change. As we discovered in the last chapter, many families are fragile and therefore vulnerable to stress. The minister is one who is often called upon to intervene in family crises and to offer representative help for the total congregation. We want now to examine the role of the minister as a family counselor, before focusing specifically on how families may go about resolving family crises such as we have been considering.

Exercise

Visit a family in crisis and assess the family's strengths and weaknesses in facing the crisis. Write a verbatim of your interview and discuss it with a pastoral counseling supervisor (your teacher, chaplain, or trained pastoral counselor may be the one to do this with you). See family assessment form in appendix.

Chapter V
The Minister as Family Counselor

*If the mission of the church is to permeate and mold
the institutions of the world, then it could be said
that a more devastating criticism of the church is not
that it is professional but that it is not professional
enough; that it is ingrown, mediocre, concerned
with the wrong things, unwise in its allocation of
resources and naive in its conception of the problems
of modern man. In short it is amateur.*
—Van A. Harvey[1]

From its New Testament inception, the church
has been concerned about marriage. After the first
generation of Christians, when Paul and the other
disciples expected the early return of Christ, Christian
congregations settled down to marry and to have families.
Strict monogamy, fidelity to one spouse, and loving care of
one's children were an integral part of the Christian life.
The sharing of all things in common (Acts 2:44, 45) did not
include spouses, although it is probable that children were
cared for by extended family members and other members
of the Christian community. The agapic ethic of responsible love suffused the relationship between spouses and
between parents and children—at least, the apostle Paul
called the members of the young churches to create this
kind of family environment. Ministry to families should,

therefore, be central to the church today. Evidence shows, however, that the majority of clergy is confused and uncertain about how best to help families. Furthermore, responsible family life committees (in the church's councils or church schools) are not completely aware of their responsibilities to parish families. Or, if they are aware, they feel poorly equipped to develop a ministry to couples and to their children.

The focus of this chapter will be on the minister as family counselor. Although I shall spotlight the pastor's key position in the church's ministry to families, I want to enlarge upon the pastor's role as the trainer of family aides and counselors. The minister cannot deal with all family crises, nor should he expect to. The optimal use of his time and expertise points in the direction of the development of a caring congregation—i.e., members who take it upon themselves to bear one another's burdens and to develop networks of caring and support both within their own group and within the geographical area where their church is located. As shepherd of the flock the pastor can extend his influence tenfold and more by working with laity as colleagues in caring, and by training them as leaders of family support groups which grow up within the parish.

1. Family Ministries

The pastor recognizes from the first day in a congregation his key position with couples and families. The congregation is made up of families at the various stages of their development. Week in and week out, these families experience accidental crisis or go through various "passages": a child is born, an elderly person dies, someone is married, someone else divorces, and the families must adjust. Widows, single parents, and divorced persons do not stand outside the ministry; they, too, need the support of the congregation and should be included within the care and concern of some family or family cluster.

Priests and ministers have officiated at the marriage of couples since the New Testament period. The early Christian era made allowance for both a secular ceremony and a sacred ceremony, a custom still followed in some European countries.[2] Couples who come to the church today to be married often return for the baptism of their first child. Literally, "a little child leads them"—i.e., the secularized couples—back to the church. Education for marriage and family living, therefore, should be a part of the minister's agenda. Ministering to couples and inter-generational groups should flourish in a supportive parish context. Studies show, however, that the average minister does not consider himself equipped to help families and couples, nor do average family life committees engage in actually supporting families in crisis.[3] The research in *Americans View Their Mental Health* (1960) reported that 43 percent of those persons with emotional problems consult with their minister first. Although the church's influence in North America has declined since then, one can say with confidence that the majority of church members with marriage and family problems come first to their minister.[4]

A questionnaire which I submitted to 175 ministers in the parish in 1976 uncovered from this group a feeling of inadequacy and lack of training in dealing with marriage and family problems.[5] Despite the fact that marriage and family courses have been a part of seminary curricula for nearly thirty years, such training has never appeared central to many—that is, until after seminary. Then pastors find themselves inundated with marriage and family problems. And then, unless they take advantage of family counseling workshops and summer courses, they will not develop the basic knowledge and skill necessary to be of optimum help to those who come to them for counsel. Moreover, pastors and church family-life committees may discover they have some limitations as to what they can do for families. My experience in teaching family counseling both at the seminary level and to ministers who are in supervised pastoral-counseling training programs has alerted me to several mistakes which the inexperienced and untrained counselor can make:

(1) He does not structure his counseling, so far as time and location is concerned; i.e., he does not move from precounseling into counseling with a counseling *contract*. As a result, either the couple or family does not make a second counseling appointment or only one family member returns for help, which makes a systems approach impossible.

(2) He is wedded to individual approaches, many times using a kit bag from a variety of psychological and philosophical backgrounds—which means from his standpoint he is eclectic, but from the parishioner's standpoint he is gimmicky and not authentic. He is amateurish in an area where he is expected to be knowledgeable. He lacks a family theory which is expressed with integrity in the practice of counseling.

(3) He is not sufficiently acquainted with referral resources—either marriage and family agencies or counselors in the community—and is not trained or comfortable in the process of referral. As a result the minister as family counselor seldom arranges for the couple or family to get help in the community that he cannot offer them himself.

(4) He may act as super-parent. The parishioner unconsciously puts the pastor into a mother or father role, and the untrained pastor takes it on and probably unconsciously (as countertransference) maintains a parent-child relationship throughout the counseling contact.[6]

In the same vein, church family life committees may perform ineffectively in their ministry to the total family within the church. For example, here are some ways family life committees may go wrong:

(1) They may continue to separate family members from one another at church, continuing the divisive tactics which go on in employment, schooling, and other community activities.

(2) They may teach a rigid religion of the law and not a liberating gospel faith which frees family members from the various idolatries. Masters and Johnson contend in their first book, *Human Sexual Inadequacy*, that theological reasons are often the underlying causes of sexual inhibitions and shame in patients who come to their clinic for treatment. I would contend that the patients they interviewed probably come from a certain kind of church where law and not gospel is the subtle atmosphere of pulpit and church school teaching.[7]

(3) They may not challenge family members strongly enough to adopt life-styles which take acount of pressing issues of world hunger, ecology, and the maintenance of world order, nor the struggles of minorities and the disadvantaged in their own communities. Civil religions and the new pietisms may preoccupy committees not sensitized to the presence and critical needs of families other than their own.

(4) Finally, such committees may have given too little care and nurture to hurting families in their midst and too little support for families outside their group for which they have a mission.

All of which points to the need for the lead minister, the pastor, to develop a family agenda within the church itself. This means not simply taking on the whole problem himself. Such messianism is out of place in the contemporary church. But rather it means the pastor must develop a vision of total family ministry and what that vision implies for the parish (or the district, synod, conference, or diocese if his responsibility implies a larger area). The pastor's expertise is as theologian in residence, with the time and training to develop the vision from within the Christian faith and its long tradition. But the implementing of this vision—even the trying it out to test its validity against the vision, experience, and understanding of other fellow members of the Christian fellowship—this waits upon the enlisting of laity in the common family ministry.

2. The Pastor as Family Consultant

The umbrella term for what a minister does in relation to members of a parish is *pastoral care*. Pastoral care is the day-in and day-out working with persons both in one-to-one relationships and in group contexts. One calls on and engages many types of individuals: singles, widowed, divorced, as well as parents, youth, and children who live in families. Pastoral care focuses on the overall shepherding role of the minister—"tending the flock" to keep the pastoral image. Contemporary nonbiblical images which preserve the caring function of the minister but which are nonparental and nonpatronizing of laity are difficult to find. However, I would suggest *family consultant*. Although this name does not reflect the authority given the pastor for his theological-interpretive task (teaching and preaching), it does communicate the flavor of what the pastor does with families.

Pastoral counseling is the specialized role in which the minister employs counseling abilities and skills to work with persons in one-to-one relationships and in group contexts, generally around a crisis situation. A lot of pastoral counseling is centered upon marriage and family problems. In fact, many pastoral counselors who work as full-time directors of pastoral counseling centers say that two-thirds to three-fouths of their clients come to the center with marriage and family difficulties. One may expect, therefore, that marriage and family counseling will be at the heart of the counseling one engages in as pastor of a congregation. The other one-fourth to one-third of the counseling one does with individuals is crisis counseling. One may conclude that if one knows marriage and family counseling and crisis counseling as specializations within one's pastoral ministry one should be able to work with most persons who come for help. The other specialized skills one needs to know as a pastoral counselor are *diagnosis* and *referral*—i.e., how to understand the nature of the problems one confronts with individuals and with members of a group (including marriage and family members); to discern if one has the necessary skills to work with those who come for help and how, when and to whom to refer. More will be said about these matters in chapter 6 when we discuss the counseling process and methods.

What then is the unique role of the pastor in the care and counseling of families? I want to use the analogy of the theater to indicate what the pastor as "chief among the laity" may do within a Christian congregation as a family consultant. The pastor is the scriptwriter, first and foremost, at times even the playwright; then, the stage manager/director of the play; the acting coach of the players; and finally the trainer of all of the above (scriptwriters, acting coaches, and stage manager/directors). The following diagram and description are useful in understanding the analogy:

1. The scriptwriter knows the *theology and story* of the church and interprets it by the principle of correlation—i.e., through teaching and preaching, the scriptwriter listens to the questions persons are asking

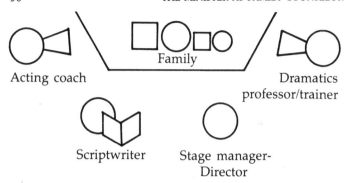

regarding marriage, divorce, singles living, conjugal living, child rearing, various new life-styles, intergenerational problems, and, through teaching and preaching, brings the Christian gospel and tradition to bear on these questions and issues. The script must be a *contemporary* script, but, like the modern-dress versions of Greek plays, it does not sacrifice the central themes of the original drama. The gospel themes are not outdated, but are brought into living dialogue with the contemporary questions.

2. The stage manager/director is concerned with developing policy and program on marriage and family life which the players are involved with existentially. The community of believers must be organized into the best educational program, and policy must be worked out so that married couples, singles, and families can learn and grow within the context of the church as a family of families. The stage manager/director role of the pastor finds expression in organizing, administering, and finding leadership for those who work in family life committees, church school programs for children, youth, and adults and general church conferences and retreats concerned with marriage and family enrichment and growth.

3. The acting-coach role is the counseling role. As a pastor, one is involved in helping couples in crises and in the passage-points which require working through to new understandings of oneself within their marriage and family system. One is also involved in providing role models in marriage and family living in one's own life within the parish. If one is married and has a spouse and family, coaching involves participating with fellow parishioners in all the pain and pleasure of growing a Christian family. If one is single or celibate this need not preclude the acting-coach role, as one participates in other person's families out of the experience with one's family of origin and finds ways of coaching children, youth, and married couples in creative growth experiences.

4. The trainer of scriptwriters, actors, stage writers, and directors helps the members of the parish to learn any or all of the above roles, including the theological interpretive role. One particularly is concerned in developing a body of knowledge and expertise in marriage and family living which has been tested in a Christian community. One finds trainers within the church and community to equip laity as family aides—i.e., persons who can work closely with groups in particular ages and stages of their lives. One becomes such a trainer oneself in marriage and family enrichment, recognizing that the experience itself strengthens one's own marriage and influences one's entire ministry. (More will be said of this role when we discuss the church as a family of families.)

3. A Theology of Family Counseling

In the remainder of this chapter we shall develop a theology of family care and counseling appropriate for both lay and professional worker within the church. One begins by stating that the primary agent of pastoral care and counseling is the *congregation*. If ministers forget that principle through their specialization in clinical pastoral education or marriage and family counseling, they run the danger of losing the primary distinction and strength of pastoral counseling. Within a Christian congregation one's fellows "laugh with those who laugh and weep with those who weep." The distinctive emphasis of the New Testament is that we are *all* "members of the body of Christ." It is the supportive network and bonding which develops within a congregation that sustains, enriches, and enables persons to become whole and grow toward new creaturehood in Christ. (We shall develop this theme in more detail when we elaborate on the church as a family of families in chapter 10.)

The pastor has a unique role among the body of Christ, what we have been calling the *scriptwriter:* he or she has a theological education and is assigned the *interpretive task* within the congregation. As teacher-interpreter, the minister correlates the questions and problems people develop in their day-to-day existence with the answers one finds in the gospel. I shall develop this methodology at some length below, but first let me put the pastor's role as theologian within the tradition of the Christian church.

The content of the gospel is that "God was in Christ reconciling the world unto himself." In that respect, whether preaching or counseling, the minister is about the business of *reconciling,* bringing the "good news" to those persons who are alienated from themselves, from their neighbors, and from God. The center of that good news is *Jesus Christ,* the paradigm of God's vulnerability, caring, and hope for humankind. By that I mean that Jesus uncovered for us God's purpose as well as embodying his nature. Jesus' ministry of teaching and healing announces the reign of God and invites persons to repent in order to

live within its community of justice and love. Jesus'
voluntary acceptance of the cross not only reveals the
vulnerability of love but also opens up the healing power
of such love—reconciling persons to God and healing
individuals' separations and estrangements from one
another. The Suffering Servant (Isaiah 53) "by whose
stripes we are healed" reveals the gracious caring structure
of God's creative order. The spirit of this love continues to
overcome the powers of darkness—i.e., sin, error,
confusion and, finally, personal death. Jesus' person and
work are the ground of human hope in that he points the
way to the new humanity; his resurrection establishes the
final victory of Holy Love over all in the universe which
would defeat its reign. His Holy Spirit counsels all those
who gather in the name of Christ and will continue his
reconciling and renewing work among and between
people until he comes again at end-time.

Now, let us turn again to theological method. How does
the minister correlate the questions people face in their
everyday existence with the content or, more specifically,
the answers one finds in the Gospel?[8] This is a dialectical or
dialogical approach and differs from a socratic or eductive
approach where the teacher draws out from the questioning learner the answers already present within him. The
individual's potential is distorted by sin and alienation and
cannot therefore be self-actualized without "conversion."
By conversion is not meant necessarily a "turnover of the
emotions" but a redirection or reorientation of one's life by
the reconciling power of God. The answer of the gospel
does not come wholly from outside the individual, couple,
or family, but there is some intervention which produces a
turning of individuals' minds from self-love to concern for
the other. The seeker finds help in refocusing, reframing,
and redirecting his initial concerns (satisfying his needs,
shoring up his defenses, manipulating others to his
desires) to understanding the deeper existential questions

which involve him with life's meanings and its more profound relationships.

Daniel Day Williams speaks of this deepening conversation as the principle of linkage and says:

Whenever we begin with human problems we recognize that what we see and feel here and now may break open for us at any time questions concerning the meaning of existence and the question of the meaning of all existence. I cannot understand one without the other. But if this be true, then the introduction of the question about God into the search for personal healing is not arbitrary. It is the moot question which underlies every other question.[9]

What links the minister to Jesus' work of reconciliation is the care and cure of souls. He accepts the couple and/or family when they feel least acceptable to themselves and most alienated from one another. He communicates verbally and nonverbally that he will work with them through their suffering until they can become connected again as free and caring persons. He names the power of love when it seems appropriate; however, much of what happens to the seekers happens by indirection. The troubled ones may need to borrow the pastor's belief in healing and forgiveness and, by the openness of the pastor, be led to discover new life rising out of pain and defeat. As John Cobb says, "When belief in God leads to the assurance that no one is beyond redemption, the pastor may have hope when other counselors despair."[10]

4. *The Correlative Cycle*

The pastor engages in a reconciling dialogue with the individual, couple or family, and it may move in a cyclical fashion to various levels in this fashion:

Counselee		*Counselor*
Question raised at trivial level	→ ←	Answer, rephrasing question (acceptance communicated
Deeper question raised	→ ←	Question placed in a religious context, universal dimension
Existential question raised	→ ←	Answer from the gospel
Response to gospel: commitment depths of existence	→ ←	Response of church through symbol, myth, ritual (naming, story-telling, celebration in play, song, rite)

One does not answer questions the family or couple or individual is not asking, nor does one plunge deeper than they are willing to go. However, rather than being passive, the pastor recognizes that the gospel word is spoken when the existential questions are asked. Prior to that the pastoral counselor helps the couple sort through distortions, blocked understandings, and bad feelings to get to the level of reconciliation. The process can be likened to the way two lovers get acquainted: they reach out, they engage in small talk, they tease and test each other, and then they may fight and confront one another seriously. At that point they begin to raise serious, even existential questions: Do you really love me? Do I love you as much as someone else? If we both love each other should we make a commitment to each other and under what conditions?

Let us now put the principle of correlation to work at several key places on the family developmental span. In so doing we can discover what the existential questions are which couples and families ask and learn how the gospel responds to those questions.

Marriage of Couple

Questions

Can I love and be loved within an intensive and sustained relationship with the opposite sex?

Is this a passion of the moment, or is it something that will last?

Is there love enough to sustain us over the long haul?

How do we get our life-styles together so as to allow man and woman both independence and mutual companionship?

Can we find some eternal verity upon which to establish our home?

Answers

Love is something which begins in an infatuation but which grows through a developing relationship.

Love requires trusting one another, but it also demands risk—going beyond immediate certainties into the unknown.

One gets life-styles together by conference, by contracting, and finally by commitment.

One's commitments are made to another but finally demand social underwriting and founding upon the structures of existence (God's creative law and re-creative love).

The church's response is the wedding ceremony "before God and the company of believers."

Birth of a Baby

Questions

What has happened to us? (Asked at the time of pregnancy in wonder and surprise)

Will we be able to nurture this child to maturity?

To whom does this child belong?

Upon whom shall we and this child depend for his growth and nurture?

Answers

You have entered into the creative process of existence and soon will become parents.

You should trust to providence that you can carry out your responsibilities as mother and father.

You are the parents of this child; but ultimately it belongs to God, and you are entrusted as stewards of this life for a period.

You both can depend on God's sustaining power and grace and the support of the family of God (the church) to help you nurture and sustain this child.

The church's response is the sacrament which names the child, affirms the child as a gift of God, and acknowledges the support of the congregation for its nurture. With dedication and youth baptism the child responds on his or her own to questions of belief and practice. Confirmation is not a sacrament but a confirming of the vows taken for the child by parents at the time of the child's infancy.

Death of Family Member

Questions

Is this all there is to life?

What kind of world is this that determines I must leave it just when I learn to love it?

How can I face the loss of my dearest ones—my parents, my mate, or my child—when they precede me in death?

Answers

There is more to life than I can perceive with my senses or conceive rationally.

Intimations of the transcendent break in on my awareness as they have broken in on the consciousness of poets, visionaries, and artists from the beginning of time.

My tradition speaks not only of birth and death but also of rebirth and resurrection.

The community of Christ circles me around when I face loss, and the spirit of the Eternal comforts me and mine despite loss and tragedy.

One should say that there are certain *Why?* questions which cannot be answered but simply must be lived with. For example, at the time of sickness, accident, or loss, people ask, "Why did this happen to me?" or "Why did God do this to me?" One can point to natural causes of an illness like infection or stress, but the individual still wonders why he suffered this fate now, this bad fortune, when others escape it, and feels as though God has turned away from him and his family. If one digs to the bottom of the question *Why?* as Job did, underneath the question is the hidden assumption that I ought to be spared the hurt and anguish that others experience. I should have all the joy of this world but none of the pain. I should not only be God's child but God's special child, to whom nothing happens that will cause me to suffer.

The Church's response: If certain things did not happen to you, you would not be fully human.

You are undergoing the suffering which all people experience at some time or other during their lives.

In suffering, pray to God for courage; in loss, pray for consolation. In death, celebrate the life of the lost one within the community of Christ and commit him or her to God's eternal care.

Conclusion

We have focused on the key position of the minister in working with couples and families. This position calls for leadership in developing an approach to married persons and families at the various developmental stages and life crises of a church's membership. *The minister is a counselor and consultant* to families. Using the analogy of the stage, the pastor is a scriptwriter, stage writer–director, and acting coach to persons within the family drama. The job is too large for one person or even a staff of professionals to perform. A theology of the laity recognizes the congregation to be the final agent of pastoral care and the clergy as trainers of laity as family aides. Moreover, ministers work within a theology of reconciliation, helping persons move from the peripheral areas to the central questions of their lives—i.e., the meaning of their existence, their ultimate commitments, and their final hopes. The correlative approach touches singles, couples, and families at each age and stage of their lives, in good seasons and in bad. When people get into difficulty they then seek out the church and the minister because both the congregation and its leader have been there right along. How does the minister help people in trouble? This will be the subject of the next several chapters. Then we shall return again to the helping role of one church member to another and to the reality of the church as a family of families.

Exercise

Develop your own theological statement as to the nature of marriage and the family. Include its created nature and purpose and the place of marriage and family within the church.

Chapter VI

Family Counseling: Structure and Flow

> *What has revolutionized the field of therapy is the realization that a goal of therapy is to change the sequences that occur among people in an organized group. When that sequence changes, the individuals in the group undergo change.*
>
> *—Jay Haley[1]*

The field of family therapy offers the minister some basic understandings of how to help family members in difficulty. Although family therapy is barely three decades old, creative innovators and practitioners have brought the state of the art to a place where ministers can employ its techniques with some confidence.[2] Pastors have been active in the establishment and current operation of the American Association for Marriage and Family Therapy, although only a minority of the clergy choose to become specialists in the field. What I propose to do in this chapter is to describe for the generalist pastor—the one who works with couples and families in the parish—the structure and process of family counseling. In the chapters which follow I will apply specific methods developed by family therapists to three kinds of family problems which every pastor confronts in the parish. I would hope that the student of family counseling would seek out a supervisor—either a trained family counselor, a supervisor with AAMFT, or a teaching practitioner at one of the family institutes—to oversee the family counseling in which he is engaged. For, in truth, a written text can only whet one's appetite and set one's directions in the field; the tutorial method is finally the way to learn to counsel with families.

1. The Structure of Family Counseling

If there is one point of agreement among specialists of family counseling, the point is that the entire family should be seen in counseling for change to take place. The last several decades have seen marriage counselors accept the fact that conjoint therapy is the treatment of choice in working with married couples. The marriage relationship is the place where the partners are having difficulty and therefore where the counseling should focus. "Marriage counseling involves understanding the social system of marriage in the family in order to counsel couples and families effectively. Marriage is a cluster of interpersonal relations centering in the rights, duties and expectations which individuals bring to husband, wife, parent and child roles."[3]

Previously, I have suggested four ways of structuring marriage counseling, i.e.: seeing the partners together; seeing both partners but separately; seeing only one partner and referring the other to another counselor; or not seeing the missing partner at all, if inaccessible. Methodologically, family therapists like to work with all family members involved in the problem. Sometimes this is not possible and the therapist may speak only with a parent or with an adolescent. Murray Bowen believes that since parents are the most powerful influences in the family, one should work with them to get change in the family system. However, many other family therapists from Gerald

Ackerman to Salvadore Minuchin believe that to influence the family system, all persons should be present. I shall follow this *total approach*, while recognizing that some members may be inaccessible, in intensive treatment with another therapist, in the hospital, or recalcitrant so far as getting involved is concerned. The mother with a postpartum depression and the brain-damaged child are two examples of family members who should be receiving additional treatment. In most instances the pastor will have contact with all family members through the church. *For the family system to be changed, all members must be involved, discussing the current family contract, with each contributing and counting for one* is the principle on which we shall operate.

How should the pastor arrange such a family interview? He can plan to hold it in the home of the couple with their children, if the intrusions of telephone, television, and visitors can be controlled. Couples with young children may find this the only way in which they can all manage to be together. On the other hand, the pastor with a large enough office can arrange to see the family there; he can seat them in comfortable chairs and locate himself within the family circle. Sitting behind a desk for an interview suggests that he will be an "answer man" and, in addition, he is not so free to move about the room or to use innovative approaches. If there are very young children they can be left at home. School age is perhaps the youngest age at which a child can interact and participate fully in the session.

2. The Process of Family Counseling

Family counseling has as its purpose helping a family to understand the role of each in the family system, what each needs and expects from the other family members, and how they can contract together to work through the problems they face and to restore the family's unity and productivity. When the family approaches a counselor for help its members have reached an impasse in their relationships, are not coping with their problems, and are in overt or covert conflict with one another, breaking the family peace. The counselor does not set out *to solve* their problems but rather hopes to open up communication between family members, to help them understand their actions and interactions which produce the conflicts, and to enable them to try new forms of behavior and role relationships which will be more satisfying to all and more productive of family harmony. Most families will be able to respond to such helping operations within ten to twelve sessions. The more difficult family problems will take longer, and the counselor is encouraged to continue with the family if he has the expertise and training to work with them. Otherwise, he is advised to refer the family to others in the community: family psychiatrists, psychologists, or social workers equipped to handle such situations.[4]

Now we are ready to work through the process of family counseling step by step:

I. **Contacting the family and forming a helping relationship.** Although the pastor may know the family superficially through other church contacts, when a parent or youth phones or talks with him personally about a family crisis or problem, he will begin by establishing a helping relationship with the individual. The pastor then invites the entire family to enter into counseling with him about the crisis or problem. This may not have been the originator's idea: he or she may have wanted to see the minister alone. Other family members may be reluctant to see the pastor upon invitation. However, the pastor explains what family counseling is to each family member over the phone or in person and sets about to become a counselor to *all* the family. When the first interview takes

place, the pastor knows other things are necessary, but
first and foremost rapport must be established with each
family member. One or another may look at him with a
jaundiced eye, or hold out from getting involved.
Establishing a trust bond with the distrustful member and
getting the holdout involved are primary goals for the
minister in order for counseling to proceed.

II. **Assessment of the family problem.** The family
counselor begins by assessing the family problem—what
has gone wrong within the family system that has caused a
breakdown in communication, the meeting of members'
needs and expectations, and the resulting problem
between family members. I use the term "assessment"
rather than "diagnosis" to stay with a pastoral rather than
a medical model. The purposes of the assessment are:

   (a) to get a clear picture of who the family is, what their
      background is, and what the existing structure of the
      family is;

   (b) to evaluate the presenting problem in each mem-
      ber's words, and the current status of each family
      member;

   (c) to gain some idea of the intensity of the family
      problem or crisis and each member's responsibility
      for it;

   (d) to establish whether you, as a counselor, are capable
      of working with the problem or whether you should
      refer the family to another helper, agency, or clinic.

In the beginning one observes the interaction between
family members, one perceives the feelings running
between them, one tries to get into the life space of each
member. One tries to understand what is going wrong in
this particular family which causes strain between them
and a breakdown of their working patterns of relationships. It is not a passive role, although one does not do
much but inquire and listen at first. The questioning is to
get family background and to establish the presenting

problem. One does not ask *why* questions, but *who, what, when, where,* and *how* questions which establish the family story and the events of the family crisis. One asks questions at the same level as the family. One does not probe too deeply, or else one or another family member will deny or reject the matter and be frightened out of the counseling process itself.[5]

1. *History taking.* One begins by taking a family history, with each family member contributing to the counselor's understanding. Virginia Satir has developed a way of doing this, starting with the parents' describing their meeting and establishing the marriage and continuing to outline the important events of the family leading to the present and the current crisis.[6] Murray Bowen has developed the *genogram* as a way of getting out not only current family history but the history of the family back at least three generations. (See chapter 3.) The counselor can construct the genogram along with the family, using a large pad of newsprint, asking questions, and drawing the family tree along with their help. All the while, he is perceiving family patterns and interactions through the genogram, which will be helpful for the next stages of family counseling.[7] Not only are the family's operating principles, their generational and personal boundaries and conflict areas described in the first session, but the genogram will enable families to find pay dirt in unscrambling the family's systems failure in future sessions. (See chapter 7.) The family's ethnic and sociocultural background will emerge in the history taking as well as its community and work relationships in which it takes part. If the family crisis is severe, this history taking can wait until later; however, it is uppermost for any family counselor to take a history. Otherwise a divorce or prior hospitalization can go unreported and skew the counselor's understanding of the current family problem.

2. *Presenting problem.* The first session should be

centered on establishing what the family's presenting problem or complaint is. Each family member will perceive the difficulty from his own position. Therefore, each should be heard from in turn. The parents may begin: "Johnny is acting up in school. What should we do about him?" One does not accept this as the root problem in the family but merely the crisis which brings them into counseling. The child will need to be heard from before the total problem is in view. Some family therapists, like John S. Bell, insist that the children speak first. He does this in order to involve them in the counseling and to prevent the parents from monopolizing the conversation. Virginia Satir and Murray Bowen, however, feel that since the parents are responsible for the child, they should speak first. Bowen, as a matter of fact, dismisses the child now, feeling his responsibility lies primarily in teaching the couple how to parent and how to work out their problems of becoming separate and mature individuals. My preference is to involve the child in the counseling since his needs and expectations count in the family, and not to wait too long before focusing on his understanding of the problem and his role in the family.

Sharpening the presenting problem is important in the first interview. Some family therapists think of this problem as symptomatic of deeper conflicts beneath the surface, which will come out as the counseling proceeds. I tend to agree with Jay Haley and the Strategic therapists who accept the presenting complaint as the one which the family wants to work on, and to keep the counseling focused on this problem until it is redefined by the family, and then perhaps do recontracting around the new problem. Although the counselor appears to be working with symptoms, focusing on the child's difficulty in school, his behavior is described by family members as disturbing both the mother's and father's usual ways of functioning in the family and upsetting the homeostatic balance of need fulfillment by all parties. The presenting problem is important, therefore, in order to get a handle on helping the family to change.

If the child is in elementary school one can use methods other than the interview to get some understanding of the family problem. Steinhauer and Rae-Grant suggest tapping the child's fantasy life and feelings of conflict by the use of puppet play; drawings, along with stories the child makes up about what he has drawn; the game of three wishes; the animal game (what kind of animal do you want to be and for what reasons?); the squiggle game (complete a meaningless line into a picture and tell a story about it); the house-tree-person (Machover) test; and the desert island game. It is suggested that the counselor get some supervised training before the use of such projective techniques.[8] If these methods are carried out by a colleague, consultation is necessary before one proceeds further in the assessment of the family.

3. *Responsibility for the problem.* Often some one person or persons get more than their share of the blame for the problem as the family tells its story to the counselor. One takes some time for each family member to own his or her share of the difficulty. The parents may scapegoat the children, projecting their own feelings of anger or guilt upon them. In order to get beyond the scapegoating and the parents' report that the problem is a rebellious child, one does not accept this as the final word. "Let's proceed a little further. Tell me about a recent incident. When Johnny returns from school and begins to raise mayhem, what happens?" The counselor then learns that Johnny just says one thing or does one thing, and all the wrath of the gods descends upon him. What happens in the home also happens in the counseling room. Johnny begins to cut up, and the parents descend on him in exactly the same way. The counselor observes the interactions and, as the

counseling proceeds, attempts to have each member accept his part in exacerbating the conflict.

4. *Family's current status.* One evaluates the current status of each family member, and of the whole family in terms of its holding together as a unit. If this is an alcoholic family, is the father drunk when he comes to the session, or has he just come off a binge? If the adolescent has been brought by parents for counseling, is the youngster in trouble with the authorities or at school? If there is an extended family problem, is it possible to get in touch with the grandparents to get their input? What crises are the respective family members going through and how are they handling the crises? Has the mother left home, threatening divorce, and what is the rest of the family doing in her absence? Is there role-stereotyping going on—with mother stuck in the housekeeping or nurturing role, and father stuck in the breadwinning and community relations role? Does each person count for one in the interview? Or does father count for one and are the others just fractions, bowing completely to his opinion? Does the family see enough value in their holding together as a unit for the counseling to be undertaken and an attempt made to get to the bottom of the problem? All of these questions are important and should be faced as one first connects with the family.

III. **Contracting.** After the assessment process one should be able to understand the nature of the family problem and determine if, as a counselor, one should undertake to work with the family. Many family service agencies at this point conduct a case conference with their staff to help the counselor determine just what the central problem is and how the problem should be handled. If one does not work on the staff of a clinic or agency, the pastor will need to decide in his own mind what the focus of the counseling will be before he begins treatment. Then, the contract is very important to spell out with the family.[9]

The contract is the means by which the counselor establishes with the family what counseling is, how it is to operate, what its limitations are, and what your expectations of them will be as a counselor. If you believe that you should see all family members, you will need to structure that into the counseling from the beginning. The family's expectations of counseling which have been expressed from the time they entered the room will need to be built into the counseling procedure. You let the family know your expertise and establish your authority as a counselor at this point. You may help them understand that the breakdown in communication, the failure to keep role commitments, the conflict between several parties as to family roles and work roles, and the misunderstanding and pain being experienced will need to be aired openly and honestly. Recontracting between family members so as better to fulfill individual needs and to reestablish family homeostasis will involve give-and-take by all parties. You let the family members know that you believe there is hope. Your entry as a helper into the situation will inspire hope, at least for the first several hours of counseling. You need to disavow magical expectations, however, of a quick fix of family troubles. The belief in a *deus ex machina* answer dies hard among those who come to pastors for help. One does not encourage transference feelings (feelings of extreme dependency) in the process of contracting. One rather explains the structure and process of counseling so that family members will understand how they are to begin to help one another sort out their difficulties and to begin again to work productively on their problems.[10]

IV. **Intervention.** Having assessed with the family what the problem is, having determined that you can work with the family and they with you, you intervene in some helpful way to break the impasse in which they find themselves. You do this actively: As a matter of fact working with *all* family members demands that you be active and direct in your approach. The particular kind of intervention depends upon where you are in the process and the nature of the family crisis and its particular coping resources. The Johari window helps the counselor understand the perceptual interaction in the family and appropriate interventions at each stage of the counseling process.

	KNOWN TO OTHER	UNKNOWN TO OTHER
KNOWN TO SELF	(Public) Formal Information Seen Appearance	(Private) Feelings Expectations Frustrations
UNKNOWN TO SELF	("Bad Breath") Attitudes Facial Expressions Body Language	(Unknown) Unconscious Motives Hidden Memories Unrecognized Potential

(a) Formal information and the family's appearance are readily apparent to each member[11] and to the counselor; this data is gathered by taking the family history and constructing the genogram. The counselor *attends, listens,* and *connects* the various aspects of the family history and background. The question and summarizing statements are the primary interventions at this point. One's presence with the family while gathering data and getting some fix on the problem has a calming effect. The family feels that now someone has entered the family system who has some objectivity and can bring some relief from the stress they have been feeling.

(b) Material which is just beneath the level of awareness—feelings which are concealed from other family members—may now be expressed in the counseling session. Frustrations, desires or response from others, expectations, guilty feelings at letting others down—these will be forthcoming if the counselor creates the climate of openness and honesty. The counselor intervenes to help the family members connect feelings with events and interactions in the family. Clarification of feelings is not intrapersonal but interpersonal. "You are angry at your mother for not standing up for you with your father," the counselor may say, connecting feelings with interpersonal events in the family. The counselor *gatekeeps;* i.e., opens up opportunity for the less verbal member to speak, and monitors the verbose member so each can express his or her opinion. In order to correct an emotionally unsatisfying pattern, each family member must *see* the sequence of events which lead to frustration. The *intervention* of the counselor breaks the frustrating pattern, allowing not simply ventilation of feeling but, in the crisis, the possibility for a different pattern of communication and interaction. It becomes then not just, "Tell your mother how you feel," but role-play how you would now like it to be different. This mobilizes the anger into a different pattern of interaction in which mother stands up to father and son feels he has some more freedom to grow.

(c) The attitudes, facial expressions, body language, and covert evaluation of others which one is not conscious of, but which other family members know about, is called the "bad breath" area. Admittedly these matters have not been talked about openly and may be the sand in the wheels of the family system causing irritation. The counselor is aware of the bad breath area of each member as the problem unfolds. Like other family members he may hesitate to inform the responsible one how offensive his attitudes or behavior are. *Confrontation* is the method of intervention. The counselor may open the situation so one or another family member may confront the offending member or, if that fails, at the appropriate time he may confront the individual. Confronting a parent with his keeping an adolescent at a child's level of dependency; confronting a youth over his defensiveness or withdrawal from the rest of the family; confronting a parent with what his broken communication does to his children—these are ways a counselor may break up a destructive pattern. One does not *interpret* intrapsychically, but intervenes in ways which can help the individual interrupt the sequence of his behavior and adopt a different stance toward other family members.

Giving "family directives" is perhaps one of the most confronting and yet helpful ways of working with this bad breath area.[12] If the mother continually interrupts the father when he tries to tell his view of the problem the therapist can break in and tell the woman to let her husband continue. If the mother has been the primary disciplinarian in the family, the counselor can give the family a directive which puts the father in the disciplinary role for the coming week and ask the family to do something in particular which will test out the father's ability to withstand his wife's interruption. This "home-work" then gives the counselor a chance to get feedback the next week on the directive and help the family to change the patterns which are causing part of the family problem.

(d) The unconscious area (unknown to self and other) is probably out of bounds to most pastoral counselors. It does influence the family's behavior, however, in the following ways. The family tends to repeat earlier behavior patterns learned in their families of origin and to do it unconsciously. Freud described this tendency as the repetition compulsion; i.e., the tendency of parents to relive their unconscious parent-child problem with their own children. Murray Bowen labels this tendency as the multi-generational transmission process.[13]

Undoing the damage done to one by one's parents—low

self-image, excessive guilt over not measuring up to
expectations, the desire to please others at one's own
expense, and so on—may require the individual to
undertake psychotherapy, which is beyond the efforts of
the beginning family therapist. Resistance to change, poor
response to family goal-setting, continuation of dysfunctional behavior by the symptomatic family member may
point to this unconscious aspect of the family problem and
indicate that the pastor may need to refer that person to a
more experienced family therapist. However, as we shall
explore in the next three chapters, the pastor with enough
training and understanding of family systems approach
may be able to intervene helpfully to work through deep
conflicts and to uncover hidden potential in family
members making possible genuine interpersonal change.

V. **Enabling.** The family counselor realizes that each
family will do the major modification of their family
system between sessions. For that reason the interviews
may be spaced two weeks apart after the initial crisis is
over. And when the family appears to be making major
modifications in their role behavior, the counselor may
move the interviews to a month apart. A vacation period
when a troubled adolescent has a chance to be away on his
own at camp may provide a real opportunity for growth
and for the family to shift its equilibrium from overconcern
for him to a better balance of freedom and control.

The counselor's role in the latter stages of helping is to
enable the family to express their new intentions in action,
to come back together after some period of practice to get
feedback on their new role behavior from others and from
the counselor. The pastor supports the parent's new
flexibility about rules, the child's attempts at sharing with
a sibling, the adolescent's shift toward responsible action
in school. Murray Bowen calls this role "coaching," and it
feels like this in practice. The family must play the game
and take the hard knocks of encounter, progressing at

times toward the goals they set and at times being set back.
However, the counselor is sensitive to their intentions and
attempts to modify behavior toward a family system which
allows autonomy for each person and interdependence of
all persons. At the beginning, togetherness may have felt
like being stuck with a bad situation and with persons
whose behavior toward you you did not like. A crisis
upsets the old balance and gives each family member a
chance to adopt a new attitude and stance toward the
others, thus modifying the family system for everyone's
benefit. There will then be a new family contract: an
understanding of what each wants and needs from the
others and is willing to give as a part of the whole.

VI. **Termination and/or referral.** The counselor concludes his counseling with the family when he and they
think the family is able to function without his support,
intervention, and enabling. If this is a parish family he
does not say good-bye to them but attempts to relate them
to some part of the church's worship, educational, and
service activities. If the family is from outside the church,
he may say good-bye to them but leave the door open if
they need to return at any time for additional help.

Family therapy allows for—in fact, encourages—referral
when it appears that the counselor is not the person to help
this particular family. I would like to suggest some
indicators which the pastor may use to help him decide
about referral or consultation:

(a) If the pastor decides upon assessment that the problem
    will take more time and expertise than he has, he
    should refer. It is better to do this at the beginning than
    to wait until he feels he is over his head and the family
    begins to distrust the pastor's ability to help.

(b) If the pastor, despite proper assessment, finds that the
    family crisis has unconscious determinants, or if one
    family member continues to have such deep-seated

problems that the entire family cannot concentrate on family interaction, he should refer.

(c) If the pastor develops severe discomfort with the family or with one family member (perhaps the family problem duplicates the pastor's own family history) he should refer. There are some family problems which the experienced pastor realizes that he is not good at. These he should refer.

(d) If the pastor is working alone and encounters some difficulty which he is not able to work through but generally he feels comfortable with the family, he may obtain a consultation with another family therapist. If this difficulty then can be worked through he can well continue with the family and not refer. Such a consultant is advised for every working family counselor, no matter how much training he has had.

Family counseling is not a "bag of tricks" but is a process in which one person lends his expertise and skills to a troubled family so that family can cope again with their problems and live together in some kind of harmony. We have explored the structure and flow of this helping operation as a pastor works with a family. What we want to do now is look at specific family situations and apply specific family counseling methods to these situations. In this way the working pastor may get some help as to how to approach situations which he confronts in the parish he serves.

Exercises

(1) Conduct an intake interview with a family, using the Family Interview form in the appendix as a guide. Plan to discuss the interview with your instructor or pastoral supervisor.

(2) If you do not have clinical opportunities, arrange with a couple to give them the Sager Marital Contract forms *(Marriage Contracts and Couple*

Therapy, Appendix i, pp. 315-20). After they have completed the forms, help the couple to make their implicit contract explicit through an interview with them. Write this up and discuss it with your instructor.

Chapter VII
Counseling the Three-Generation Family

> *Each family we treat contains a part of our own. As I*
> *saw more and more families I have become used to*
> *reliving each stage of my own family life cycle*
> *during sessions, in a series of flash-backs at once*
> *compelling and fearsome, fascinating and despair-*
> *ing, growth-promoting and regressive.*
>
> —*James Framo*[1]

The three-generation family is not very American. Although the prevailing opinion is that the extended family was strong in former times but has given way recently to the nuclear family, facts prove otherwise. Mary Jo Bane conducted a historical survey of the family in America and concluded that "the nuclear family, consisting of parents living with their own children and no other adults, has been the predominant family form in America since the earliest period on which historians have data."[2] She adds, however, "that although few extended families have existed in America, families have always expanded to take in needy members . . . but fewer older people and people in disrupted marital situations now live with their families than did thirty years ago."

Other research points to the fact that the proportion of three-generational households is dropping. Fifty years ago in the state of Massachusetts 50 percent of the households included at least one other adult besides the

parents. Today that figure is 4 percent—a 46 percent drop.[3]
The reduction of family size, the move of families to
metropolitan areas, the loss of neighborhood networks—
all these trends have continued to work against intergenerational living.

The tendency in middle-class America is to isolate the
older generation into retirement villages, nursing homes,
and convalescent wards. If the elderly are from the lower
class they are put into mental hospitals, state farms, and
cheap hotels (halfway houses). In most cases these places
are "warehouses for the poor" and register the neglect
which children heap upon their aging parents. It is not
mentally healthy for the older generation to be completely
divorced from the younger. Such isolation and lack of
contact with younger people produces apathy, the feeling
of being useless and worthless, and, in severe cases, an
early death.

What I propose to do in this chapter is to present the
context of intergenerational living out of which problems
arise, to analyze these problems in general terms before
presenting a three-generation family as an illustrative
case. Then I shall proceed with some methods of handling
this case and conclude with some counseling approaches
to use in working with three-generation families.

1. The Context of Intergenerational Living

What happens when three generations live under one
roof? The Chinese have a proverb which states: "One
woman in a kitchen is happiness; two women in a kitchen
is disaster, war." The younger woman can never cook in
the right way. The older woman knows it all and is
continually telling the young woman that she is not doing
it right and implying that she is not a good cook. Many
novels and short stories in the Orient center on this kind of

generational conflict between mother-in-law and daughter-in-law. A triangle is formed between them, and they battle over the son and husband whom they both love and do not want to share with the other. The clannishness and cliquishness of this kind of family shuts out the person who tries to enter its portals. Marriage poses a threat to the bonds which have been tightly wrapped around children during their growing-up years.

Murray Bowen describes this kind of situation as *fusion*, an emotional "stuck-togetherness" which prevents children from differentiating themselves from parents and continues an overdependency into a new marriage. The poorly differentiated young adult will subconsciously seek out a mate at his same psychological level and, rather than entering into a relationship where each may fully develop his identity, will *fuse* with the mate, losing self in a submissive position. Such an individual, if living under the same roof or within easy traveling distance of home, will continue to look to his parents for direction and advice, and create turmoil with the mate who gets caught in a power struggle for his allegiance and loyalty.

The first critical point at which fusion becomes evident is at the time of the marriage: parents don't want to let their young person go but still consider him or her to be their child and loyal first to them. The son may find it easier to disengage from his family than the daughter. However, in certain ethnic situations either son or daughter is expected to come back every Sunday to the family home and to consider his family of origin to be his first loyalty. The second critical point is at the birth of the first grandchild. Grandparents have been waiting in eager anticipation for this moment. It is a moment of great pride and one in which they can enjoy the child without full responsibility for him. Difficulty may arise over the discipline of the child. There is a sense in which grandparents always think of the new parents as too lenient. At least they are not following the same child-rearing practices which their parents did. When grandparents countermand parents over discipline, parents feel undercut in their authority over the child—in fact, they feel like children themselves again. With three generations under one roof it is difficult to see how this situation will not obtain.

What happens when the three generations live apart? Although they live apart, the older generation can still attempt through gifts of money or taking over the care of children during holidays or summer periods to dominate the parenting generation. Fusion may still take place, although what the younger couple may attempt to do now is to use geographical distance to create enough emotional room for them to grow independently. When young couples isolate themselves from their parents, run away from them to another part of the country or the world, and deny their emotional connectedness to them, they are involved in what Bowen calls an *emotional cut-off*. Minuchin calls this a *disengaged couple*, as opposed to an *enmeshed* one. The disengaged couple has overreacted to rigid parents or rejecting ones and separates themselves so drastically from them that they may not see them from one year to the next. When they left home they cut themselves off from their parents and had no idea of giving credence to anything the parents would say from then on. This is the rootless family which moves from the old homeplace to a large urban center. They do not want to go back home at all. They have shaken the dust off their shoes from that place and vow never to return again. But as Bowen and Minuchin point out, the disengaged are no more free from their parents than the fused couple—and repeat the parents' mistakes on their children.

Three generations can live under one roof, but it takes some contracting at the time the young couple moves in with the parents—if they decide to do this before starting a household of their own. It requires some talking through at the time aging parents decide to move in with their middle-aged children at the time of retirement or the death of one of them. This contracting is done openly and at some length at the time the new living arrangement is being made. If couples have difficulty with the contracting they may wish to talk to a family counselor or get the issues resolved. Here follow some principles for such contracting as two or three generations attempt to adjust to group living:

1. Maintain the generation boundaries with some flexibility. In other words, grandparents realize that they can counsel their children, but that the new parents have primary responsibility for their children and should be allowed to exercise it. However, the second generation should be willing to listen to the older generation when their wisdom is shared with discretion.

2. Allow for interchange between the generations. When a young couple marries, they should have responsibility for major decisions—even when they live under the parents' roof. When an elderly couple moves in with their children, they too should be allowed to exercise authority over their lives. In the interchange over grandchildren, mutual respect for one another should be the context of discussion even when opinions about discipline differ. Parents should have final authority in these matters, even if the older generation believes them to be making a mistake.

3. Each generation should have their own space, their own belongings, and a sense of privacy from one another. It is when the young and old lack privacy that problems arise. Minuchin reports problems in a family which arose primarily because no one ever closed any doors and privacy became impossible both for parents and for youth.

4. There should be festivals and occasions for family celebrations for all generations. Birthdays, holidays high and low, anniversaries are necessary in order for families

to cement their bonds, to let their spirits rise, and just to have fun together. Christmas, Thanksgiving, and summer vacations may then become times when the good will and love between family members can be expressed and reinforced.

2. A Multigenerational Problem
Gary and His Grandmother[4]

A. Setting and Background

Gary, who is twelve, is an attractive looking blond-haired boy of average height and weight. He lives with his grandmother, who is fifty-two, slightly built, and dyes her hair black. Mrs. M. has had two sons; one is married and lives in the next town.   The other son, Gary's father, divorced when Gary was an infant. The wife did not want Gary. Gary's father remarried shortly after the divorce and had a new family. Gary was not wanted here either. So Gary has been living with his grandmother since he was about one year old. He is now repeating sixth grade.

Gary and his grandmother live in a small one-bedroom walk-up in a heavily German-American neighborhood. Gary sleeps on the back porch. Mrs. M's first husband died, and she remarried about ten years ago. The marriage to an older bachelor did not work out, and now they are separated. Mrs. M. now has a boyfriend who occasionally takes her out. Gary is jealous of the time away from him, and makes disparaging remarks about his grandmother and her boyfriend. Gary sees his step-grandfather often and seems to have a good time with him. Mrs. M. is jealous of this relationship, but is also glad to be relieved of him for an afternoon.

The counselor (a woman) works with Gary in the evening youth fellowship where he really stands out as a difficult child. He dislikes group activities and usually refuses to cooperate. Instead he will hit the girls, try to grab the ball in games, and generally disturb whatever the group is doing. He is very good at playing the handbells, which the group does for about fifteen or twenty minutes each Sunday afternoon. After a few sessions, however, he refused to play with the others. The same is true of art. He can be very artistic but gives up after a short time in group projects. In order to keep him out of trouble the counselor asked him to do some project for her like moving books. He appears to want to be the center of attention in whatever he does, and when he isn't, he tries to bring attention to himself even if it is a negative response. On the other hand, the counselor has found him to be a very attractive child. "He can be very caring toward his grandmother, assuming a masculine role of protection toward her," the counselor said. "I have tried to get to know both Gary and his grandmother by visiting them two Sunday afternoons. As part of my position as youth minister I am expected to contact families and to arrange lunches with them. I invited myself over to Mrs. M.'s for lunch." The following verbatim is a portion of that second visit. The goals of this visit were to understand their situation a bit better and also to support Mrs. M. in some of her difficulties. She has been out of work and has been looking for a job all winter. In addition, she has been in poor health. After some chitchat at the beginning of lunch, the following conversation took place:

M-1   We got up early this morning and made sure we got to church. Gary wanted a friend to stay over, but I said: "No. We have to get up early this morning. Besides your friend is being taken care of by his older brother. I don't think he should be over here then. His parents will expect him home."

C-1   So you really put your foot down?

M-2   It used to be very hard to be firm with Gary. But this was necessary. Things are getting better.

Gary's marks were poor this past term, and I wouldn't let him out after school for ten days. I just had to be firm.

C-2   You feel good about that?

M-3   Yes, it's better for Gary. Our situation is better now . . . "knock wood" for the future. Of course, I don't have a job, but I'll be looking this week. *(At this moment Gary runs in, wet from the rain which started as he was coming home.)*

M-4   Gary, you're all wet. Change your clothes or you'll get a cold. Your grandfather will be here soon!

C-3   Hi, Gary!

G-1   Oh, hi.

M-5   Change your clothes.

G-2   I'm not that wet. I'll just take off my coat.

M-6   Gary! *(Shouting)*
       (Gary makes no response. He disappears into his room in back.)

M-7   *(Muttering to herself)* Sometimes I don't know what to do with that boy!

C-4   *(Seeing his door open, I go to his room. He is looking at his coins. He has a nice collection and is very interested in them.)* Could you show me what you have there, Gary? *(Gary responds enthusiastically, describing the various values of each coin. This goes on for about five minutes. Then a bell rings. It's his grandfather. Gary puts his coins away and puts on a dry jacket. He runs out. I return to the kitchen.)*

M-8   He'll be with Mr. M. for the afternoon. . . . We went together for five years before we were married, but I guess once a bachelor always a bachelor. He lives with his sister now. I guess Gary was too much for him. He said it was O.K. when we married, and what could I do? I couldn't leave that child! It was O.K. with Mr. M. in the beginning, but it got too much for him. And my family! All the directions! Everyone knew exactly what I should be doing!

C-5 It was difficult being a wife and parent again.

M-9 Yes, he was only about a year old when I got him, but he's a good boy. He calls me "Mom"; I really like that.

(Telephone rings. Five-minute conversation. She is excited and giggly.)

M-10 That's a friend. We're going for a ride this afternoon. He's borrowed a car, and we're going to take a nice spring ride.

C-6 That sounds nice. I hope this weather cooperates.

M-11 No matter what the weather is, we're going to have a good time! I've told Gary that if he wants to come when we go out like this he can and can also bring a friend, as long as the friend isn't a troublemaker. But I just have to get out! I've been cooped up here in this apartment most of the winter. Since September I've had one thing after another. First shingles, then bronchitis and asthma, and finally the flu. It really made me depressed. I found I would be crying over nothing. My doctor told me I needed to relax, and he gave me tranquilizers. That's when he told me I should try to get a transfer at work. I was getting anxious over the job. The manager was getting harder and harder to work with. But the only opening was in Philadelphia. I couldn't take that! Yes, it was hard this winter. I would be arguing with Gary a lot because I was so cooped up. Things are better now but I remember I was so mad at him one time, when he just wouldn't listen, that I hit him. That really surprised him!

C-7 That really surprised you, too?

M-12 Yes, I guess so, but he was just so aggravating that day . . .

C-8   How did you feel when you hit him?

M-13   Oh, I don't know. I think he deserved it, but I
        certainly wouldn't want to hurt him.
        *(Telephone rings again. Her boyfriend is on the line. The
        rest of the conversation reverts to chitchat.)*

The family genogram would look like this:

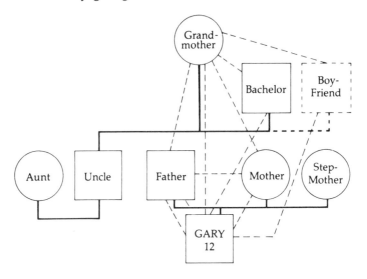

1. *Fusion.* One can hypothesize that Mrs. M. was fused
with her son; it certainly existed between Mrs. M. and her
bachelor husband. There is also fusion between Gary and
his grandmother. As the counselor reports: "Mrs. M. is
Gary's grandmother, mother and, in some sense, girl
friend. She confides in him and needs his masculine
protection. . . . Though she resents her responsibilities of
being a mother to Gary, she also seems to want this role to
herself. Her signals are probably confusing to Gary, often
creating a feeling of instability for him." This is especially
so as he enters adolescence, is aware of his sexual feelings,

and feels guilty for leaving grandmother for another girl. The impression one gets is that there is a multigenerational programming for fusion/cut-off, and that it is now becoming evident in Gary's behavior.

2. *Cut-off.* The way in which the family handles fusion is to cut off and abdicate child responsibilities. Gary's father cut off from his grandmother and turned Gary over to her. Gary's mother, about whom we know little, might have taken him, but she also cut off. Gary's grandmother has had two husbands and has cut off the most recent one. She has not abdicated her responsibilities for Gary, but she is not handling them well. Her symptoms show up in her relation with her manager at work.

3. *Triangles.* One is able to understand the insiders and outsiders through looking at the triangles in the family. The early triangle was between Mr. M., Mrs. M., and Gary. The new triangle is between Gary, the boyfriend and Mrs. M. Gary tolerates his step-grandfather better as a visitor—as Mrs. M. does also—than as an in-house relative. However, of more interest is the triangle between Gary, his father, and Mrs. M. This is the basic relationship to look at and to try to help both Gary and Mrs. M. to handle.

B. Theological Analysis

There is an estrangement between Gary's natural parents and Mr. and Mrs. M., and the failure of reconciliation between these parents extends to the failure in parenting in all those persons involved. As the counselor interprets the situation: "The estrangement in the marriage relationship has fostered estrangement in her relationship with her grandson. . . . This is one more time a parental figure either deserted him or made him feel he was a burden and the cause for estrangement. Because of this estranged state, Mrs. M. cannot forgive either Gary or God for putting her in this situation." The counselor continues: "Mrs. M.'s idea of God is one who will take complete responsibility for her future, giving her companionship and security, without asking much in return. Gary's God will provide him with complete emotional maturity and companionship without asking for much in return. There is no way to get to reconciliation and forgiveness. God is an extension of ourselves."

Another way of saying this is that the grandmother reacts to her current situation childishly and to God with both childish dependence and petulance when her prayers are not answered. To be reconciled with God she must seek some reconciliation with her son and a better resolution of her interpersonal difficulties. Gary can be expected to be confused with his grandmother and incapable of finding his identity as God's child because he has such a tentative identity as a grandson and none as a son. Counseling will be helpful for him before his confirmation experience where the intellectual dimensions of his faith are sorted out.

How should the pastor work with Gary and his grandmother? Assuming that this is the opening wedge to the family, the pastor should state to Mrs. M. that he wants to work with other members of the family in order to unscramble the messages Gary is getting from everyone. The purpose should be stated that the counselor wants to get to know each person in order to understand what stake he or she has in Gary and what responsibilities he or she has unloaded on Mrs. M. Once counseling has begun the pastor would ask for Mr. M., the "bachelor grandfather," to come in to talk about Gary's behavior. He has Gary's confidence, and, even though he no longer lives in the home, his weekends with Gary give him some leverage in helping Gary through this difficult period.

In the counseling Gary's needs should be counterpointed with his grandmother's needs and Mr. M's needs, with some balance found satisfactory to all. This would be a working substitute now, but since the divorce Gary wonders just where he is with everyone and if these signals do not mean he will be passed on to someone else. Mrs. M. should give Gary some reassurance that she does not plan to remarry and that, if she were to remarry, neither Mr. M. nor she will abandon him.

Mrs. M. should be encouraged to contact her son, Gary's natural father, who abandoned him earlier. The son should be invited by the counselor to come in with them as a consultant for Gary's sake. The long-term breach in mother-son relationship and father-son relationship should be addressed. Gary's father should be encouraged to affirm Gary in the future as only his natural parent can affirm him. It may be suggested that occasional visits be set up between Gary and his father and that the father may wish to remember Gary at birthdays and holidays.

Gary and his grandmother will need to work out issues of separation and support to enable Gary to develop an interest in the boys and girls at school and at church. Gary has been an emotional ballast to Mrs. M., even a substitute partner at times. He now needs room to become more independent. And she needs freedom from him to sort out her job, her emotional relationships, and her private life. Finally, Gary needs additional youth activities to further establish generational boundaries between himself and the adults around him. Perhaps the pastor can suggest a summer camp away from the home where peer activity is prominent and intensive. Were the pastor to be a counselor at such a youth camp, he or she might further follow his progress and counsel him through some of his difficulties.

This is not a short-term case but one in which I should see some hope of change were the counselor willing to work with the family over the next period of months. Much depends, as it has in the past, on the strength and flexibility of the grandmother, on Mr. M.'s willingness to do more, and on Gary's native intelligence and capacity to respond to loving care and support.

3. Counseling with Multi-generational Problems

There are two different ways of working with multi-generational problems. The approach the counselor takes depends on whether he or she is working with a fused, overly rooted family or with a cut-off or thinly rooted family. Granted that, as in the case discussed above, some families will be both fused and cut off, after the family appraisal one can determine one's strategy and plan appropriate interventions.

A. The Fused Family

The fused family is the three-generation family where the stuck-togetherness needs opening up so that the new parents may proceed with their living and nurturing activities with relative independence. The counselor begins by asking the grandparents to come in for a consultation with the family. He does not communicate any blame to them but calls on their wisdom as parents to help with the current difficulties. But this time their "advice" is made in the counselor's presence where it can be moderated and filtered somewhat. Carl Whitaker, who has shifted his practice toward what he calls "Four Dimension Relationships," describes such a consultation: "The content of that interview may be purely social, or merely supportive. . . . It certainly need not involve content of any significance. . . . It merely serves as a time when the parents meet this man who's going to replace them, and develop some willingness to turn over to him the care and nurture of this child."[5]

The goal of the interviews is to help the new family "to

become free to separate and thus free to belong"—to use Whitaker's phrase. In order for that to happen the generational boundaries will have to be reestablished so that the nuclear family can develop sufficient independence to parent their own children. In-law problems are not the product of individual nastiness but result from parents' clinging to their grown children and the grown children's inability or unwillingness to cut loose from their parents. One helps the older generation to let go of these young adults and the new couple to "talk up" to their parents and to "grow up" to their adult responsibilities. Bringing the generations face to face allows both groups to perceive their current living situation more correctly and to understand where their primary loyalties lie.

Establishing generational boundaries should enable grandparents to act like grandparents and parents like parents. Being a grandparent means giving up primary nurturing responsibility and allowing the new parents to carry this out independently of them. However, this does not mean the support system between the generations is abandoned. Such a consultation should make grandparents, parents, and children aware of such support and willing to call upon it appropriately.

The new parents should learn how they are trying to create the family of origin in their family. As counseling proceeds, the counselor intervenes in such a way so that the new parents get free of the patterns learned from their parents so as to create a new family nexus. To be sure, certain ideas about discipline, the spending of money, and roles in the family will continue; however, a new mix from the mother's side and the father's side should emerge, given time and circumstance. Allowing adequate time to communicate the background and traditions of each and to establish parental roles which fit not only their personal needs but their partner's expectations is the focus of the latter stages of counseling.

B. The Cut-Off Family

The cut-off family is probably more typical of intergenerational problems. The parents and grandparents are cut off from one another geographically at the time of marriage and the new family is just as problem-oriented as the old family. Something within the life process calls for meaningful separations and, when they are not made, both families suffer. The rootlessness and the breakdown in family traditions and family values are felt in the new family as a lack of structure and a network of support. Children neither know grandparents nor have the advantage of knowing exactly where they spring from as a family.

To counsel such a cut-off family, the pastor should begin by making the family conscious of its roots. Constructing a genogram (see chapter 3) will make them and the pastor aware of their cut-offness. They, no less than the fused family, are trying to undo the mistakes which they think were made in their parent's handling of them. The necessity of making contact with this family should become clear to them in the early stages of counseling.

The counselor supports the reestablishment of communication with the cut-off parents or, if they are deceased, with the most well-functioning aunt or uncle, and certainly with siblings if they are outside their ken. If these persons live at a great distance, the couple is encouraged to write letters, inquiring as to the health and current activities but, more importantly, taking up with the individuals when the communication breakdown or disagreement occurred. The response to such letters becomes a part of the interviews, the counselor coaching the couple as to their follow-up efforts.

Murray Bowen has developed what he calls a "family voyage"; i.e., a sending of the adult clients home on timed visits to living parents or aunts and uncles and siblings who can talk with them about the events of the past. The purpose of the visit is not only to reconnect with one's relatives, but to become aware of the family patterns which one carries over to one's own parenting operations and to become more differentiated as a self. Ways one relates to one's mate and works out roles, ways of bringing up children and establishing homeostasis in one's home are now possible of understanding and correcting through the counseling. The cut-off is then able to get on with the business of becoming a more independent person and a more responsible marriage partner and parent.

Finishing unfinished business with one's parents, siblings, and other relatives should enable the couple to establish a healthy emotional distance again with them. One's family has a "forever-extended time dimension," says Carl Whitaker. The new family will have to relate to their parents even though they have moved to another city and no longer live in close proximity. The counselor helps the couple to finish the unfinished business and, in the ensuing months, to maintain contact with extended family to keep the relationship alive. Finding the generational boundaries which allow sufficient emotional distance for independence but enough connection for support will be the concluding phase of such counseling.

Counseling cross-generations is highly important to the pastor and to the church. The writer of II Timothy addresses the reader to the "faith which was alive in Lois your grandmother and Eunice your mother before you, and . . . lives in you also (II Tim. 1:5 NEB). Faith, traditions, and values are passed down from one generation to another. Distortions in that generational sequence not only break the psychosocial sequence but cause a breakdown in faith held and values practiced. Renewing and restructuring the generational sequence will allow the next generation to claim its faith and to find its values.

Exercises

(1) Listen to Murray Bowen's tape, "Differentiation and the Family System." (Can be obtained from California Family Study Center, 4400 Riverside Drive, Burbank, CA 01505.) Discuss family systems from a cross-generational perspective with your instructor.

(2) If possible, interview a family with three generations under one roof. Pay attention to the flow of the conversation, the fusion, and cut-offs within the generations.

Chapter VIII

Counseling the One-Parent Family

*Up until recently, the whole issue of families was not
one in which people had to make hard choices. Now
people have more options—to get married or not, to
have children or not, to stay married or not, to work
or not. These options are really at the heart of
everybody's concern.*

—David A. Goslin[1]

Sue was upset. The school bus had left school
without her. She was intent on going camping this
weekend with members of her class and now she would
not be able to meet them at the rendezvous point. Her
divorced mother worked, so she could not help her make
the place on time. Disappointment flowed over her as she
began to cry. It was just like her to foul up. She blamed the
school for giving her so many things to take home that she
could not make it to the bus on time. Who would take her
home, she wondered. She missed the bus so often last year
that her teacher told her she would not take her again. She
was running out of those upon whom she could call.

My wife and I picked her up with all her books and
clothes and took her the five miles back to her home. On
the way home, my wife spoke of what a radiant child she
had been when she first knew her five years before. That
was before her parents divorced. Now she was a confused,
mixed-up, and awkward adolescent. She tended to

impose on people and certainly was searching for attention. But more than that, she wanted some structure—someone there when she needed him who could help her out of the ordinary mix-ups young girls have. And finding no one at home, she was becoming more of a problem at school than the other girls in her class.

Sue is just one of the many children in the United States who will live in one-parent families before they are eighteen years of age. There are today one million widows with children under eighteen and two million divorced females, nine-tenths of whom have custody of the children of the marriage. The most recent statistics show that almost half the children of the United States will experience the loss of a parent before they reach maturity. One sees the immensity of the problem when one considers the increasing number of divorces of young parents thirty and under.[2]

In addition to the extent of the problem, we need to look at the nature of the problem. Following this overview I want to present a case study of such a one-parent family in order to understand how a pastor may best counsel in such a situation. Finally I want to present some counseling approaches which a minister may use with widowed, divorced, and blended families.

1. Description of One-Parent Families

In this chapter we are dealing with families in which one parent is attempting to raise children on his or her own without a second parent. The statistics show that most parents who lose a mate through divorce, desertion, or death continue to parent the children of the union rather than giving them up to the state for adoption or placing them in foster homes. Mary Jo Bane reports, "The data suggest that the proportion of children who live with at least one of their parents rather than with relatives, with foster parents, or in institutions has been steadily rising."[3] The ties of blood are too strong for most middle-class parents to give up their children to relatives, even though, because of working, they may now lack time to give them sufficient nurturing attention. Moreover, lower-class homes, particularly among blacks and ethnics, will keep the child within the family although there is more of a tendency to turn over the parenting responsibilties to a grandmother—as in Gary's case—or to an aunt or a sister. Often there are problems when this occurs, particularly when the loss of the divorced or deceased parent is not acknowledged or worked through with the child.

The grief process must be worked through by remaining family members whether it is the death of a family member or loss through divorce. The spouse will naturally grieve and experience the hurt of the loss of his or her mate and the confusion, anxiety, and guilt which follow death or separation. Murray Bowen cautions that a "network of underground aftershocks," such as psychosomatic disorders, accidents, school failures, and other social dysfunctions can occur in the extended family system in the period immediately following such a loss.[4] This shock wave will usually cause the family to avoid and delay grief and to handle the children poorly at the time of the loss.

The remaining parent experiences an imbalance in the family system. It is difficult to parent the children without one's spouse. A mother often lacks the self-confidence necessary in making a living or in managing the family finances. Even though her husband may have handled less of the parenting responsibilities, now she has no one but herself to handle these responsibilities. The bereaved mother may be so caught up in feelings of loss and guilt at her part in the separation and divorce that she is insensitive to the child's pain and unwilling to help him through it. The father, left with the care of the children, may find himself at a complete loss. He usually is so involved with his job and so inexperienced in child care that he lacks confidence in himself to carry on alone.

The effect of the loss of a parent is different for children in the case of death than in the case of divorce. Children experience death as final, but they will continue to see the separated parent through visitation privileges. Nevetheless, the child experiences the broken circle of the family and is insecure, often wondering if he will also lose the parent who remains. Research has been carried out mainly on the impact of the loss of a father upon boy children. The effect appears to be greatest upon preschool boys. When they lose their father by death or divorce between ages four and seven they are found to become less aggressive, more dependent, and to have more feminine patterns of interest and play than boys the same age from intact families. Girls, on the other hand, who lose their fathers at ages four to seven will not show the effects of the loss until they enter their teens. E. Mavis Hetherington found that

adolescent girls who had grown up without fathers repeatedly displayed inappropriate patterns of behavior in relating to males. Girls whose fathers had died exhibited severe sexual anxiety, shyness, and discomfort around males. Girls whose fathers were absent because of divorce exhibited tensions and inappropriate assertive, seductive, or sometimes promiscuous behavior with male peers or adults.[5]

The loss of one's mate and the grief recovery process is experienced in three phases, says Phyllis Silverman: (1) Impact, in which the surviving spouse receives the news of the partner's death but goes on in numb, automatic behavior in order to manage the details of the funeral and of his or her family, job, and daily life. (2) Recoil, in which the reality of death strikes the bereaved spouse and in which he or she slowly begins the process of grieving.

Erich Lindemann originally postulated this would take six weeks, but with a family it probably occupies most of a year. (3) Recovery, in which one begins to let go of painful memories of the loss and to rebuild one's life.

Parents can help children prepare for the father's or mother's death; however, only the event itself will make death real. Muriel Fisher told of how her husband was able to break the news of his dying to their fourteen-year-old son at the hospital while she found it impossible to speak to their thirteen-year-old daughter while shopping. For the seven-year-old boy the best she could do was to let him know the rest of the family would be there and would give him support through it all.[6] The parent who survives needs to be aware of the child's grieving and rate of recovery. Eda LeShan points out that such grieving involves sensual and visual images of the lost parent, fear of what is going to happen to him, a feeling that loving is dangerous, a fear of losing the parent who is still alive, feeling angry at the parent still alive, a feeling of relief after a long illness, and a need for a substitute parent.[7]

Divorce involves more complications than the death of a mate, although the divorcing couple needs to be aware that the feeling experienced is similar to that caused by death. In addition, the couple will need to decide how to divide family income and property, the custody of children, visitation rights for the nonparenting spouse— all of which involves the law and the courts. Each partner must face the adjustment to being single again, and the children must face a home with an absent parent. We have examined above the impact upon boys and girls of the loss of a parent. The remaining parent has the obligation not to let the hurt and anguish of separation embitter the child against the other parent. Divorce, even though more frequent today, still goes against the conventions of a community, and children may suffer the taunts of their playmates. Inadequate finances may be a problem for the mother left with a family. She will probably not be paid as much as her husband at her job, and child support may be inadequate. LeMasters reports that at one time or another 40 percent of divorced fathers are delinquent in child support payments.

The problems which one-parent families may exhibit reflect the imbalance in the family system that does not have the second parent and the reactions which various family members make to right the imbalance. Let me mention three such problems which we shall deal with below:

(1) The remaining parent may attempt to make one of the older children into a parent to fill the gap left by one who has gone. The "parental child" breaches the generation boundary and may succeed to a certain extent in being mother or father to the children. However, the other children will resent him and rebel against his orders, and he will sacrifice a large part of his childhood in order to fill the parental role.

(2) The imbalance in the family system may push the remaining parent to enter into a romantic liaison before his grief work over the loss of his mate has been accomplished. This liaison may involve a conjugal partnership, as in the case below, or a marriage. Children may push their parents into such a partnership, yet resent the new person once the mother or father begins getting serious and talking about marriage.

(3) Once a new or blended family is established, stepchildren, adopted children, or foster children brought into the new union may develop problems which complicate the harmony of the family's living together. The new family will need to establish its own balance; parenting will have to be shared where before it has been carried on by only one person, and children will have to accept the new mate as a parent and the new children as siblings. One can see the endless possibilities for friction

and disharmony which are available and which will call on the best efforts of all parties in the family to work out a new accommodation.

2. *A Single Parent, Her Lover, and the Children*

The counselor, an Episcopal priest, knew Betty as a parishioner. She is a widow whose husband has been dead for four years, leaving her with three children, a boy ten, a girl eight, and a girl six. She is forty, very attractive and youthful in appearance and manner. She is friendly, talkative, artless, and open in manner. She has a high-school education and works as a bookkeeper.

She and Jim have been friendly for over two years. He is also forty, handsome, dresses casually, and is also friendly and talkative. He has a high-school education and works in an institution in a nonprofessional position. He is separated from his wife, she seeking a divorce. He is Roman Catholic, but now attends the Episcopal church with Betty. He has one daughter, eight, who lives with her mother.

Eighteen months ago Jim moved to Betty's home. In order to "disguise" the live-in arrangement, he took a room down the hall from Betty and pretended to be a boarder. This fooled the older children for about six weeks, but now only the youngest girl still holds onto the myth. Betty and Jim say that they consider themselves married in every way except for the legal ceremony, which they will undergo the minute the divorce comes through.

In the initial phases of counseling, the priest had the couple work on the Sager marital contract. After they had worked out their individual summaries they came back and worked another hour and a half talking about their expectations, needs, and desires for the relationship.

What follows is a summary statement as written by Betty and Jim.

Betty:

Marriage for me is a sharing of life's joys and sorrows with someone I love and who loves me in return. I want complete loyalty, trust, and fidelity. My mate would be first in my consideration, but it would be necessary for him to really care for the children so that we could be a complete family and function as such. I would want him to set the example and to be the head of the house. But on a financial level I feel we should both work together so that the whole strain isn't on one person and we would have more extra money to do the things in life we enjoy. Basically when I'm down, I like knowing I have someone to turn to. I really need that loving reassurance. Intimate relations should be a mutual happening but there will be times it doesn't coincide. I feel at these times we should meet one another's needs as best as possible (just be loving). I want to feel safe and secure emotionally with my mate and have him feel the same about me. I feel he lets me down when he feels really low and finds it necessary to take off for hours and comes home when ready, intoxicated. I really feel let down. I realize this is an outlet, I know he's only drinking, but I resent it, for myself first and then the children. It's a very poor example.

My psychological needs are for love, trust, and security, and I get that from my mate. I feel free to live my own life-style. I think my mate is a fine person, enjoyable to be with. I definitely like his looks. He positively turns me on. Our sex relations are very compatible. No problems. I need to be able to be myself. Fear of abandonment is a prime concern for Jim. He's afraid, and he overreacts to arguments. I don't feel free to lose my temper or get mad because he will overreact. We can't even discuss things reasonably without his becoming very insecure. We need to feel more secure in our relationship. What I am willing to give is love, trust, security, compassion, understanding, and family togetherness. I will try to respect Jim's need for thinking things out for himself. Sometimes I need time for myself. When Jim goes off on one of his trips, I pray he gets home safely and for the next day or two possibly talk about it. For myself, I take aspirins and try to go to sleep.

Our problem areas are communication, sex, and drinking. I want him to be more patient. He wants one-word answers. That's hard to do. I'm not a lawyer. My mind cannot work like

his. I try. I want him not to overreact to my slightest
disappointment. Better yet, not to try anticipating my reactions
and telling me how I feel. I want him to drink at home if
necessary. Drunk driving is out. I want him to get rid of that
stony attitude where there is no communicating. It usually leads
to his drinking. I will try to meet him halfway and better in the
things I do that annoy him. To be there to meet his needs and to
share our ups and downs together.

Jim:
   From this list the things I want are a mate who will be loyal,
devoted, loving, and exclusive. I want a relationship that will last
until death do us part; there is no other way. I want insurance
against loneliness. This is the most important thing for me (all of
the above). Next most important is the need for inspiration and
hope to carry on. Something to live for. The third most important
is sex, two maybe three times a week. A home with roots and ties
is also very important. The single life is no good. There are
financial advantages to being married and you have a better
social life. What I will give: I will try desperately to be loyal,
devoted, and loving. I will protect her against anything.
Positively I would never abandon her. I am willing to have sex
two or three times a week. I am willing to love and accept her
children as my own (I do). I will work and support the family for
the betterment of all. We all need inspiration to carry on.
   The psychological needs of myself are being met by my
spouse, and I think or feel I am meeting hers. She has a need for a
husband figure which I think I meet. She has a need for a father
figure for her children which I think I meet. She has a need for
someone to fall back on for support which I think I fulfill. I am
receiving *all* her support in regard to being a father and husband.
I can count on her to back me up and be there when I need her for
an emotional crutch concerning life in general. I am never lonely,
never without sex, never without love, never want for a hot meal
or clean clothes. She is part of me. I don't feel my spouse has let
me down in any field. She is just great: good shape, nice
personality, very good head (brains), good housekeeper, good
mother, good wife. She turns me on real strong! She wants sex a
bit (little bit) too often. We have no sex problems except this.
   I feel pretty safe and secure at present. If I am not secure it is
because she does it. There are damn few things I don't want to
share with her, but there are times far and few in between that I
do go off alone and prefer it that way.

The counselor listened to the couple as they read their summaries and worked with them toward a preliminary contract understanding. They both agreed that they find their sexual relationship satisfying, but the problem is how often to have sex. According to Jim, Betty wants intercourse every night, but he is not up to it. Then she gets mad when he says he is tired or isn't in the mood. The counselor suggested that he might feel embarrassed by not being able to perform sexually, and he began to express feelings of inadequacy and threat. Betty became angry and said, "When he's in the mood, it's fine, but when he is not, my needs don't count." As the discussion went on it became clear that what she wants so frequently is not going all the way necessarily, but someone to snuggle with in bed and to be affectionate and attentive. Jim was clearly misunderstanding this. The separate bedroom arrangement was discussed and how this led to separation and episodic sex. This is satisfying Jim much better than Betty. Nevertheless she is the one who insists upon it.

Upon questioning by the counselor, Betty went into the reason for the "boarder" arrangement. When they first met at a Parents Without Partners meeting, Jim told her he was a widower. This went on for two months while he won her affection as well as that of the three children, her parents, and all the neighbors. At the end of two months the children suggested that he move in with them in their spare room. He had been living in a dismal room in the house of an old woman in a different neighborhood until then. With this invitation he told them the truth—that he was divorcing and not a widower. This hit Betty very hard. She considered herself a strict Episcopalian and wanted nothing to do with divorce or divorced persons, and here he was not even divorced. However, upon thinking it over, she decided to invite him to live with them anyway.

He moved in; however, his official status was the "boarder in the spare room," and Betty was not about to change that until they were married. I asked her if she thought anyone was fooled by this. "Only the six-year-old child," she replied. The other children all know the score and seem to accept it. Everyone loves to have him—parents, neighbors, children. The priest-counselor thought that Betty was operating on a code of ethics that says sex outside of marriage is wrong, but if you are committed to be married, it is all right to jump the gun. Thus the behavior was episodic gun-jumping and not the conjugal bed. At the end of the discussion both Betty and Jim appeared to think that when they married and were sleeping in the same bed the quality of the sexual relationship would be better for Betty. Jim appeared to be relieved that it was not increased quantity that Betty wanted but more affection.

My appraisal of the couple's situation would include the children's situation. Both Betty and Jim want Jim to be father to her children. The "boarder" arrangement is secretive and undermines Jim's authority as a potential father. How the couple communicate with each other before the children is now setting the structure of future family relationships. Needless to say, the live-in arrangement means that Betty no longer has a one-parent family. But she is uncertain as yet just how Jim will function as a parent to her children. They like him as a boarder; he is probably permissive and does not have to discipline them in any way. The "secret" between Betty and Jim needs to be shared with the children, and this probably will not be possible until they announce their plans to marry. Then the next phase of adjustment of the children to a new father can begin to take place.

There are several steps the counselor can take when the divorce becomes final. He should see Betty and Jim in a series of premarital counseling sessions to plan for the marriage. Making a final commitment to each other will change the live-in arrangement and should include some understanding of parenting responsibility to their children—Jim's daughter by his previous marriage and Betty's children. Will Jim want to adopt them, or will he want to wait until later for this decision? The counselor will want to have the children come in with the couple to talk through their feelings about having a new father. The live-in arrangement has prepared them for some of the practical aspects of having Jim in the house, but relating to him now as a father and the spouse of their mother will require them to make some shifts in their thinking. Finally, the counselor should arrange to see the couple after the marriage to follow up the new family in their adjustment to one another. How is Jim handling his role as father of Betty's children? How are the children adjusting to Jim as a new father? And how is Betty adjusting to having Jim not as a boarder but as a husband? If there are triangles or cut-offs or scapegoating one should be able to pick them up in this post-marital session and work with the couple around the incipient problem before it becomes an entrenched pattern.

3. Counseling Methods with Single Parent Families

The pastor comes into contact with a single-parent situation every time there is a death of a parent in a parish family. He will be called upon to help the family at the time of the funeral. Today's trained pastor can be expected to counsel the remaining parent through the grief situation. I want to present here some additional ways to be of help to the entire family at the time of loss. And further I want to discuss ways to help with the eventuating problem—the parental child—the child the single parent puts in the father's or mother's place.

A. Adjusting to the Loss of a Parent

The pastor uses supportive counseling with the grieving parent and helps him or her go through the normal grief process. Parents Without Partners, Widow to Widow programs, and church support/growth groups will be of help to single parents in the early stages of grief. However, the counselor's attention should be focused not only on the parents but also on what is happening to the children. Here his role is to "coach" the parent to be sensitive to each child and to provide emotional support so that the child can adjust to the loss. The parent can take time to listen to the child's fears and insecurity about the loss, to help the child reach out to other relatives, particularly sisters and brothers of the dead parent, and to stand by the child as he has difficulty with school or with his friends. The child may not be in grief counseling; however, the single parent can be "coached" as to how he should be handled as he, too, works through his grief.

In the case of divorce, children should be prepared for the separation before it happens. If the pastor has been involved with the couple in marriage counseling, he should continue to see them right through the divorce period. I agree with Richard Hunt that each phase of divorce counseling represents a distinct crisis and should be faced with a different agenda.[8] What often is left out of such counseling is attention to the children's reactions. Here again the counselor "coaches" the responsible parent in communicating with the children. Louise Despert lists four guiding principles to help one with children of divorce:

(1) Acknowledge that there has been a decision to separate.
(2) Acknowledge that grown-ups can make mistakes and that his parents have made them.
(3) Assure him that he is in no way to blame for what has happened between his parents.
(4) Finally and most important, assure him in every way possible that, despite your differences with each other, you both still love him as you always have.[9]

The pastor may intervene quite actively in a one-parent family to help find a parental substitute for the children. A person in the parish—married or single—may be discovered who is willing to give some extra time toward helping the single parent with parenting. Gary's step-grandfather in the case above liked the boy and was willing to take him to athletic events or simply for a drive. Without such surrogate parents the surviving parent may find himself overwhelmed with his responsibilities and prone either to overprotect the children or to deny them legitimate parental guidance and help.

B. The Parental Child

One inevitable way a parent may fill the gap left by the loss of the partner is to make the child into a parent substitute. Salvadore Minuchin has helped us understand the difficult position such a child occupies. He shows by a structural diagram how this child breaches the generational boundaries.

Therapist   <u>Mother</u>   ⋮ Parental Child

                                      Children

Many times an older child or adolescent can assume the position of parental child without too much apparent stress. However, the problem arises, Minuchin says, "if the delegation of authority is not explicit or if the parents abdicate, leaving the child to become the main source of guidance control and decisions."[10] Such children find it impossible to control the other children, are tense because their childhood needs are not satisfied by anyone, and more than likely displease the parent, to boot.

The pastor intervenes in such situations in order to change the structure of the family so that once again the parent can be the parent and once again the child can become the child with his siblings. The generational boundaries are reinstated with the counselor's help.Minuchin is a master at this, using geographical space as one means. He positions himself between parent and parental child to break up the previous structure. He recreates communication channels, shutting off the child when he talks like a parent, and turning only to the actual parent for opinion on discipline matters, for instance. He challenges the parent to the obligation of making family rules and sticking to them. He marks boundaries so that the parental child becomes aware that he is expected to find his satisfactions in being a child again. He assigns tasks between sessions for family members, putting the parental child in with his siblings and helping him get back into this role in the family. Meantime he coaches the parent to assume the responsibilities that the parental child gives up and to find someone else—a housekeeper, relative or friend—to help him with them. The pastor can do all of these things in guiding the single parent to make structural changes in the family so that the child does not have to assume the responsibilities of the lost parent.

The single-parent family is one of the fastest growing social phenomena in North America. These families are in evidence in and around every parish, whether in the city, suburbs, or open country. The pastor needs to see his obligation not simply in helping persons through the crises of death and divorce but also, through support and active intervention, in continuing to work with families who must adapt their family system to function without this significant member.

Exercises

(1) With your class, view the videotape of Murray Bowen's "Death in a Family" and discuss the problems of the one-parent family.

(2) If you have a pastoral assignment, interview a family following the loss of one of the parents and, if possible, make an audiotape of the interview for discussion with your pastoral supervisor.

Chapter IX

Counseling with Adolescents and Their Families

> *The family will change, but it will also remain, because it is the best human unit for rapidly changing societies. The more flexibility and adaptiveness society requires from its members the more significant the family will become as the matrix of psycho-social development.*
>
> *—Salvadore Minuchin[1]*

Betty's parents were away on a long-planned-for vacation trip to Europe. They had asked Laura, a young woman who lived next door, to house-sit and to get the meals for Betty, seventeen, and the other three children, who were fifteen, twelve and ten. Betty helped Laura with the meals and was most excited about having a birthday party for her friend, John. She invited a dozen close friends by phone and word of mouth. Imagine her shock that evening when scores of young people showed up bringing their own beer and wine and lining the streets in front of her home. Not knowing what to do about the party crashers, Betty phoned Laura's parents and they and Laura went up and down the street telling the crashers to go home. This worked to a certain extent, but at 11:30 a neighbor, hearing the noise outside, called the police to clear the rest of the street.

This actual incident illustrates that parents can protect their children from alien influences and values until adolescence. But when children enter junior high, the outside world invades the home in ways previously unsuspected. Drinking alcoholic beverages, smoking marijuana, and having illicit sex may be the activities most feared by parents of youth. However, these are symptomatic of the fact that the peers with whom one's young people socialize may come from homes and families with entirely different value systems or, as Bronfenbrenner and others imply, from homes where youth are unsupervised and left to fend pretty much for themselves.

Adolescence itself is not a problem, but it is a stressful period when a young person undergoes biological changes which occasion a different kind of relationship with parents. Previously dependent, he reaches out now for new independence; formerly content within the perimeters of the home, he now needs space to grow and opportunity to try on the roles of an adult. Each youth matures at his own rate; and, depending on his age, place in the family, and the type of community in which he lives, he may go through these changes with little rebellion. Nevertheless there is little doubt that his peers will become more influential than his parents and that his values will be in flux as he develops more independence from the home.

Research has uncovered certain new material which is helpful to someone who is counseling with youth and their parents. First, Erikson's theory of the *moratorium* which youth place on making final commitments continues longer than at first thought.[2] As a matter of fact, as we discussed in chapter 3, the research of Daniel Levinson and his associates concluded that this moratorium continues through the twenties. Young people are eager to make short-term commitments regarding work, place of residence, college, and friends but may want to put off marriage and to be financially dependent upon their parents while in graduate school—all of which plays into the fear of commitment and the difficulty in sorting out values which many youth bring into the counseling room.

Second, the counter-culture movements of the late sixties and early seventies appear to be over, but the effect upon the relationship between younger and older generations is still very much in evidence. Debate goes on as to how much of a generation gap there is; however, some researchers conclude that the gap between classes of young people has closed. Daniel Yankelovich says, on the basis of a study completed in 1974, that the action has shifted from campus to the mainstream.[3] Non-college and high-school youth have accepted the values of the college youth of the late sixties. One sees this particularly with respect to sex, work, and religious values.

Non-College Attitudes	*1969*	*1973*
Would welcome more acceptance of sexual freedom	22%	47%
Casual premarital sexual relations morally wrong	57	34
Relations between consenting homosexuals morally wrong	72	47
Having an abortion is morally wrong	64	48
Living a clean moral life—important value	77	37
Religion is an important moral value	64	42
Patriotism is an important moral value	60	40
Believe that hard work always pays off	79	56
Would welcome less emphasis on money	54	74

The Sorensen report on adolescent sexuality indicates that in the 13–19 age group 52% (59% boys, 44% girls) have had sexual intercourse before they reach twenty.[4]

Third, young women show the influence of the woman's movement, some of whose values collide with the values of parents. Many parents do not speak to their children about birth control or abortion and are surprised to find a daughter adopting a liberal attitude toward these issues. A daughter who has finished college may delay marriage and choose a career much to her mother's regret. And those daughters who do marry may not choose to settle into a traditional partnership like her parents and may defer having children or choose not to have them at all.

Finally, the Strommen studies of church youth find many of them not espousing the theological doctrines of their confirmation studies but holding to belief systems at odds with their church. He found in an ecumenical study (N = 7,050) that only 30 percent embodied the four characteristics which might be viewed as held by the most religiously committed youth.[5] The others might attend church or pray but practice their religion in an extrinsic (other-directed) fashion. The counselor of youth, therefore, needs to be aware of the religious struggles of young people as well as the fact that some of them are conforming to adult expectations, but biding their time until they can be on their own and believe and practice what they want. The need for a mature faith is present, but a sensitive counselor may be needed to help the young person verbalize his or her struggles to reach it.

At puberty a young person will experience conflicts with the parents which have previously been unacknowledged or unresolved in childhood. The mother and/or father may attempt to keep the adolescent at an earlier stage and be unwilling to let him grow up. Menstruation and the first seminal emission signal growth changes which the parent neither acknowledges nor makes the necessary changes in himself to accommodate the youth's struggles to grow up. Parents may not recognize the youth's need for peer approval or the need for spending more time with his friends. Arguments over clothing styles, the movies he sees, or the television programs he watches reflect the generation gap. Refusing to recognize the youth's appropriate demands for autonomy may lead to a breakdown of communication between the young person and his parents, with the youth now telling his or her parents nothing.

When parents become insecure about the youth's behavior they may become rigid rule-makers attempting to control his every move. A question like the time to come home from a party may become an area in which parents show such anxiety about a youth's behavior that they will overcontrol and overreact to unconfirmed suspicions. This distrust may drive a young person into performing the suspected act since "mom and dad don't trust me anyway." Another way in which parents may handle their insecurity is to breach the generation boundary and try to be one of the kids. Adolescents generally suspect such parental "childishness" and feel betrayed that they no longer have an older and wiser head to which they can turn. The parents will need to develop rules and maintain boundaries with the youth's cooperation, which means walking a fine line between freedom and control.

A pattern often seen by the counselor is the attempt parents make to relive an adolescent problem which he or she did not resolve a generation earlier. Transactional analysis has alerted us to parent games like *Uproar* and *Now I've Got You*, which betray parental anxieties around behavior with which the parent still has difficulty.[6] The youth gets double messages from the parents which he does not understand. The parents say either in words or acts, "I got involved in this trouble, but don't you dare do the same thing!" The adolescent may become entrapped by the parents and subjected to too much rage and reaction and become altogether puzzled by the parent's erratic behavior.

Finally, parents who are locked in a marital conflict with each other may scapegoat an adolescent and pour on him the heat of the conflict. Triangling, which we discussed in a previous chapter, is an oft-repeated dynamic in adolescence. This becomes the means by which the teen-ager may bear the symptoms of the family, as we shall observe in the case study which is discussed below. The parents can keep the conflict hidden so long as the youth continues to be sick or to act out. When the youth changes his behavior, the family homeostasis is interrupted and the parental conflict may be uncovered.

1. *A School Phobia Problem*

The pastor saw the mother, Catherine, and her daughter, Mary, on the request of the school counselor. Mary had developed a fear of attending school. The mother was 5'5", thirty-two years of age; the father was a foreman in an electronics parts plant, and was 6'2". The mother appeared to be the dominant one in the family. Mary was thirteen and had begun to menstruate and to develop physically.

Mary's fear of attending school had started at the beginning of the fall; she was not able to get to school before ten o'clock. She would be ill until 9:30 A.M.; her mother then would take her to school and she would attend for the rest of the day. Mary revealed that she disliked her home-room teacher, M. M., and that the arts teacher did not tell her what the assignments were the first day, causing her to become anxious because she was not prepared. She also did not want to take physical education as it involved undressing to take showers.

The counselor asked the mother and daughter if they had discussed menstruation and if they would mind going to see the family doctor. They set up an appointment.

Mary and her father were close. The father was staying home because of a strike at the plant. Mary tried to please her father and thought that he needed her there to soothe his anxiety. At school she was able to forget her father's problems. The counselor asked the father to come in for counseling.

Between the first and second session the counselor saw

the principal and asked if Mary's schedule could be rearranged so she could attend her best classes during the first two periods.

When Mary and her mother returned, the counselor dicovered that the mother had been going to the principal, to the mental health clinic, and to other clergy with her problem. The counselor contracted that he be the only one to see them and that they confine their counseling to him.

Mary was counseled to sit in the principal's office to calm down when she first went to school, thus eliminating home room. She was given positive reinforcement about attending the first two classes.

Then it was discovered that she had displaced her fear of school to Sunday school. She did not like to attend because her mother made her wear a long, ill-fitting dress and the other students laughed at her, she said.

At the next session the counselor saw the mother and father together. It became apparent that the mother dominated the discussion and was in control of the family. The mother was overreacting to Mary's school problem. Every night she would grill her about what had been going on. The next morning she couldn't push her out the door. She felt manipulated by the daughter. She said she was not close to Mary, and yet she took the entire blame on herself for Mary's problems.

The counselor saw Mary alone, and she talked about several anxiety-producing exeriences: (1) A holdup man was chased by the police in a shopping center she went to with her mother. She was afraid the holdup man would kill her mother. They went together to an Octoberfest and saw two men following them down a street. Again, she was afraid they were going to hurt her mother. At her grandmother's she feared someone was going to break into her room and kill her mother. The counselor did not interpret these accounts; but Mary's hostility toward her mother, and her fear that her mother would be removed from the scene before Mary was able to get all from her that she needed, appeared obvious to him.

At the end of six weeks Mary was going to all her classes. She was also going to Sunday school in clothes she looked good in. Her first marks came out; and she had received three As, 2 Bs, and 1 C, failing only the one course she had not attended. Mary wanted to tell the counselor first what her marks were, even before she told her parents.

Her mother was now resistive to coming. She resisted, in particular, talking about the mother/father relationship. When the mother's overinvolvement with Mary began to diminish, the poor relationship with the mother and father stood out as something they needed to look at. Mary responded with anxiety to the threat of the dissolving relationship between her mother and father. The anxiety had been displaced onto school and Sunday school.

As this counselor's supervisor, I helped him understand that Mary's school phobia was masking the conflict between her mother and father. Together, we planned a strategy which would enable Mary to attend school, while at the same time allowing the mother to express her anxiety directly to the father. The father's participation was vital in order for him to assume a more active role in parenting Mary and to cope with the anxiety his wife felt in their relationship. As David Lynn observed: "The adolescent with a chronic school phobia may be more attached to Mother than to Father. . . . Clinical investigations of school phobias have traced some of them to the child's jealousy of the mother/father relationship. In these cases the child fears what might occur between Mother and Father during absence at school."[7]

2. Counseling Methods

The pastor may become involved with a youth's problem through contact with the youth, through a parent's bringing the matter to the pastor, or through a school referral, as in the case above. Having the entire family come in to see the pastor should be insisted upon forcefully. The temptation is to see the youth alone, but this builds a barrier between the pastor and the parents, setting the pastor up as a "good guy" against the mother and father who are the villains of the piece. Identifying the problem at the beginning as a family problem and insisting on seeing all family members tends to prevent this kind of polarization. One may choose to see the youth alone at times and the parents alone at other times. But this is a part of the counseling strategy and does not detract from the goal—to change the family system from dysfunctional to functional.

The type and complexity of youth problems are so many that one has difficulty in focusing on a few. I want to concentrate, however, upon three: triangling, scapegoating, and social acting-out behavior, so as to highlight several counseling methods which we have not yet discussed.

A. *Triangling*

All children get involved in triangles with their parents but adolescents in particular are susceptible to such triangulation. Such a triangle is not simply sexual (an oedipal triangle), as Freud observed it, with the youth wanting sexual possession of the parent of the opposite sex to the exclusion of the other parent. Triangles involve fusion with one parent, making the other parent the odd man out. One parent is overinvolved with the youth, and the other parent is underinvolved. Power in the family is in the hands of the adolescent and this parent, and they control the family's affairs.

Such a family is out of balance, so that what is needed is to disengage the overinvolved members and to allow a new

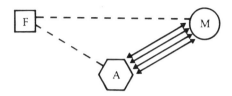

balance of forces to come into play. How does one de-triangle such a family in counseling?

Murray Bowen wisely counsels that one stays out of the triangle as a therapist and keeps the activity going between family members.[8] In other words, one does not get "hooked" (involved in countertransference operations) with any family member but attempts to open up communication between all parties concerned. "Family sculpting" may be a way to open up such a triangled family. Peggy Papp explains this method by saying that one begins by having each family member sculpt the family problem as he sees it. She calls her method "family choreography"[9]—she wants each person to be in motion in the family tableau without speaking to the other. Then each family member sculpts the family as he would like it to be. This new situation can de-triangle the fused and excluded members and allow for there to be a new constellation of members within the family.

The purpose of the de-triangulation is to allow the underinvolved parent to assume more responsibility with the youth and the overinvolved parent to back off so as to allow it to happen. The young man, for example, who relies more on his mother than on his father for conversation and role modeling will need to be encouraged to look toward his father as the father makes tentative steps toward him. The father can help such a youth by remembering some of the difficulties he went through as a youth: the trouble he had getting his first date, beginning his first job, or wrecking a car. This may come out during the conjoint session. On the other hand, the counselor may need to encourage the father in private sessions to remember how it was when he was a youth and to empathize with his son.

B. *Scapegoating*

More has been writen on "family scapegoating" than almost any other topic in family therapy. Virginia Satir calls a child who is the victim of scapegoating the "identified patient" who she says, "is saddled with the burden of believing that he actually does hold his parents together. He learns that he can unite them in some fashion, at least, by getting them to focus on him."[10] Like the scapegoat in the Old Testament sacrifice, this child becomes a sin-bearer; i.e., his symptoms are the point at which the dysfunction of the family is made visible. This skews the family and focuses the disharmony on one person when it should communicate to the entire group that they all have problems.

The counselor will therefore be chary about seeing such a youth at the parent's insistence to "fix" his behavior. Such behavior often masks the husband-wife conflict as in the case of Mary above. Seeing parents and youth together makes it possible to get the pressure off the youth and to unmask the conflict between the parents. Lynn Hoffman speaks of scapegoating as a homeostatic cycle. The father may be anxious about his work and flash the signal to the family; the child tries to help the father by staying home from school; the mother reinforces the child's phobic behavior by insisting on taking the child to school by car—and the pattern is established. Hoffman says, "In a family the mirror-image disagreement may be beneath the parent's concern for the symptomatic child, or it may appear as an antagonism toward him, but a persistent effort to get each parent to express his attitude toward the symptom will usually cause the disagreement to appear."[11]

The counselor needs to move directly to get the adolescent off the "hot spot" by coaching the parents to defocus the child. This upsets the family balance—in fact, it may make the parents anxious—but it will give the counselor opportunity to stress therapeutic goals which will provide new homeostasis. In the case above, de-triangling the youth gives her some chance to get back to school and to cease functioning as the scapegoat on whom the mother has focused and in whom the father has chosen to confide about his job anxiety. The parents are provided an opportunity to talk about the problems between them which are causing both of them anxiety. As the parents attend more to each other and less to the child, the counselor will help them to become less fused and more able to function realistically in marital roles.

Satir points out that once the pressure is off the youth, he is not only relieved but may become a helper in therapy. He can begin to function as a normal adolescent with his own needs to be met and allow his parents to solve their problems without his serving as a "sin-bearer" for them.

C. *Acting Out*

Although I shall not deal in detail with social "acting out" or delinquent behavior on the part of youth, it is only fair to spell out briefly the way a family counselor approaches such problems. Stealing, vandalism, sexual promiscuity, taking illicit drugs, and running away from home are extreme problems with which every family counselor must deal at some time. Such problems come to the attention of school authorities and the police; however, a pastor may be asked by such authorities to counsel with a family who encounters such problems. The approach is the same as we have been describing, although the crisis has made it necessary for the community to come between the youth and the family. The youth often has not been able to ask for help in words and "acts out" his despair through an antisocial act. He is saying to his family, "Please pay attention to me and provide me the parenting which I so drastically need!"

David Lynn reports: "The father of a delinquent boy is often characterized by alcoholism, criminal record, extreme aggression, brutal punishment, negligence or rejection of the boy, erratic discipline and absence from the home. In short, he is a totally unacceptable model for his son. . . . Unloving, punitive, authoritarian fathers tend to produce dependent, withdrawn, anxious, and dejected children."[12] Similarly, young adolescent girls who become sexually promiscuous, get involved in vandalism, illicit drug-taking, and eventually run away from home want very much to be loved and accepted by their parents, but act out their despair when they feel rejected by them. Alienation from parents lies behind much delinquent behavior by young people.

Reaching the parents of such youth may prove impossible for the pastor. It may be necessary for the community to place such youth in foster homes where they may have a chance to redirect their lives. But as communities such as David Wilkerson's in Pennsylvania and the Agape Community in Washington, D.C., have demonstrated, a combination of strong controls and empathic acceptance do bring many youth back to more constructive behavior patterns. Working with the parents is another matter. The pastor is obligated to visit in the youth's home and to appraise the extent of the parent's responsibility for the youth. If he can ally himself with a social worker with whom he can make the most helpful intervention to correct poor or improper parenting, he may stand a better chance of helping in the situation. If this is a first offense on the part of the youth, the pastor can perhaps help the family explore what went wrong, the crisis the youth experienced, and how the entire family may take remedial action. Haley's phrase, "giving directives," properly describes the approach a pastor may take in giving homework to a troubled family in a way in which they can take hold. A pastor as a person of authority may be able to interrupt a transaction between a youth and a parent which has caused difficulty. However, once such homework is assigned, the counselor must ask for a report of how the youth's changed behavior affected him and how the youth's response to the parents was changing the parents.[13] The counselor will reinforce the changed behavior if it has proved satisfactory to the family and will reassess the difficulties if the parents and/or the youth were unable to carry out the homework. The theory behind this kind of behavioral work is that it has been the youth's behavior which has caused problems; therefore, one works with the actions of both youth and parents to get some change in the family systems.

The pastor needs to be aware of good referral resources in the case of delinquent youth with whom he comes into contact. Sometimes the situation is simply beyond him with respect to working with drug addiction or various kinds of acting-out behavior.[14] In such cases it is best to have some knowledge of the social agencies which work best with parents and youth with these problems, and to make a good referral, keeping in touch with the family every week or so after the referral. The church's membership—at least some of the lay workers who work best with youth—should continue to be in touch with the family. A youth group may visit a young person in a reformatory or prison, for example. My experience has been that this can be the ray of hope the youth needs to bring him back to the community with some chance of rehabilitation and getting back into contact with persons and groups who will continue to believe in him and give him a second chance.

In the film *Saturday Morning*, a group of about thirty

senior-high students gather for a week-long encounter group with two psychologists. They come from the inner city and the suburbs and are black, white, and Mexican-American in background. In the early part of the week they all talk about the hassles they have with their parents about drinking, hours to come in, the clothes they wear, and the length of their hair. Toward the middle of the week they get seriously involved with one another and debate their values about having sex with a casual date, about intimacy and identity, and about what they want to do with their lives after school. It is not until the last day—Saturday morning—that they return to speak of their relations with their parents. One by one they recognized that their parents really love them—but how difficult it is now to express their love in return. More important, one young man recognized his own selfishness and how at this retreat he had miraculously broken through his shell and been able to reach out and love another person. Another participant is forced back into her shell by the leader; she cannot love her parents, she has been too damaged by them—and she is just waiting until she is eighteen and can leave home and not see them again. It is difficult to see the film and not be moved to understand what a significant opportunity parents have to be the guarantors of youth, how tragic it is when these relationships fail, and how redemptive it is when they succeed.

Exercises

(1) View the videotape by Virginia Satir entitled "A Family in Crisis," paying special attention to the way in which Ms. Satir relates to each member of the family. Discuss the identified patient role of the teen-ager and the methods the therapist uses to involve the whole family in the problem.

(2) If possible, and if a videotape machine is available,

role-play a parent-adolescent problem with which you are dealing. Review the role play with your instructor or supervisor to understand your counseling approach. If you are part of an advanced class, use the videotape to record a counseling session with a parent-adolescent problem. Review the tape with your class, allowing each person to comment on your method and the instructor to evaluate your approach.

Chapter X

The Church—
Family of Families

A crowd was sitting round [Jesus] and word was brought to him: "Your mother and your brothers are outside asking for you." He replied, "Who is my mother? Who are my brothers?" And looking round at those who were sitting in the circle about him he said, "Here are my mother and my brothers. Whoever does the will of God is my brother, my sister, my mother." Mark 3:32-35 NEB

The tear in the family fabric in Western society should stand out in the reader's mind by now. Parental absence from the home; isolation of families from their relatives; failure to teach children values; and instability resulting in school failure, delinquency, and alienation are apparent in the counseling case studies. Our thesis has been that the nuclear family is too small, too isolated, too lacking in roots and support networks to carry the emotional freight for parents and children today.

Experimental life-styles, such as conjugal living, group marriage, and rural communes, while interesting, have not proved adequate in that the persons involved for the most part have not been willing to adapt individual life-styles to the demands of cooperative living. The time eventually comes when persons who "do their own thing" give up on the others if there are no social sanctions and long-term commitments. What appears needed is not a return to the traditional family structures of former decades, not a beefing up of the nuclear family, but some alternate family structures which allow for the supportive network which was characteristic of the extended family. Provision of emotional supplies, responsible care of children, intergenerational interdependence, and development of roots and rituals call for family clustering and neighborhood groupings greater than the nuclear family can provide.

Much of what will be said in this chapter can be applied to various community organizations like the YMCA, YWCA, neighborhood houses, and social agencies which have cross-generational populations. However, I shall structure the discussions around the church as the family of families. The church, while not at the center of many communities nor as influential as it once was in many towns at the beginning of this century, has an important place today in family life. If its leadership proves sensitive to family need and flexible in its response to help families help themselves toward responsible and interdependent living, it can in truth become "That community which causes people to remember who they are and where they are going" (Carolyn Bradt).

1. *The Church as the Family of Families*

The primary agent of pastoral care and counseling is the congregation. We established this principle as rooted in the New Testament and we found theological basis for its implementation when we discussed the role of the pastor in chapter 5. Let us now discuss the congregation in more detail as an extended family and point to its function in providing care and enrichment for today's struggling families.

First, the congregation attempts to connect its members to one another in love like brothers and sisters of a parent God. Jesus Christ is the Elder Brother whose love for the church was demonstrated in his earthly ministry and in his death on the Cross, and whose care and counsel continue through the work of the Holy Spirit in its midst.

Second, the congregation through its ministry of word and sacrament brings people into living dialogue with its origins and its Lord and equips them for mission in the world. Helen Caplan, a layperson, looking at this aspect of the church's life, says:

It has been observed that the discipline of reciting a liturgy and of carrying out formalized acts at regular intervals imposes an order on an individual's life that is of continuing therapeutic value. The fact that such observances are repeated at regular intervals steadily reinforces the message of discipline, structure and identity. It regularly renews community contacts and devotion to that group's ideals by repeated exposure to signs of fellowship as behavioral scientists have discovered a constant flow of physical and social supplies and stimulation to maintain their well being.[1]

Third, the congregation recognizes its need of continuing forgiveness and reconciliation as a fellowship of reconciled sinners. John Wilkenson, to whom I owe a great deal in pointing out the centrality of the laity in the healing ministry, says:

The congregation is made up of those who once were spiritually sick but now have found healing and strength in God. They have found forgiveness and have been restored to that fellowship with God which is the aim and completion of all Christian healing. Such reconciliation is a tremendous therapeutic force.[2]

Fourth, the congregation is a fellowship whose members express their concern for one another in prayer, intercession, and strengthening one another through visitation when sickness, loss, or other distress over-

whelms a family member. The empowering spirit behind
the church as a family of families is not good works but a
common dependency on the caring and sustaining power
of God.

These roots of family life need cultivation and some
general understandings of family horticulture. The church
needs to organize itself along traditional ways of meeting
family needs through Sunday worship, but it also needs to
respond to specific family needs at various places along the
developmental cycle, as well as to plan various intergenerational approaches to strengthen these connections and
support bonds. The diagram on page 171 shows such
congregational care and concern.

We use the same correlative method developed in
chapter 5 but within the context of the church as family of
families. The questions couples and families face are
confronted in group contexts with other parents and their
children. These groups try to create the ambience and
fellow feeling of a healthy family. They can be brought
together for a short term around crises families face, such
as the birth of a baby, the wedding of a family member, a
divorce in the family, retirement of one or both parents,
illness and death of a family member. Or the groups may
be organized for a longer period—a year or longer—and
meet for the discussion of growth and developmental
issues which family members confront as they live in the
same household. These issues are family discipline, sex
education, choosing meaningful life work, recreation, and
the various community issues: schools, government,
housing, race relations, and so on.

The church responds, as do other social institutions, to
the specific interpersonal problems that all couples and
children face living in close contact. However, the church
through its central identity as the family of God rests on
the caring and supportive structure of Providence. God is
not seen as an unmoved Mover but as a loving, dynamic

Regular church program

Family worship
Pastoral care
Christian education for all age groups
Social action and social service

Marriage — Pre-School — Adolescent — Empty Nest — Retirement/Death
Birth of Child — Elementary Child — Young Adult

Family Needs

Original Family

Separation ——▶ Experience as grandparents and care-givers ——▶ Participation in intergenerational experience

New Family ——▶ Enabling support ——▶ Changing in parenting—recontracting as spouses
Infant care support
Understanding support
Become original family & begin cycle again

Intergenerational needs for connection and support
Church's response: both short-range and long-term groups to meet these needs.

Power, creating new opportunities and new choices for each generation. Within the Christian tradition such a power is known as *Holy Love*, dependable and trustworthy in his relations to a people. The church's response, therefore, is unique and should be understood by families for what it offers them. The church is an extended family, intentionally designed to relate to persons as brother to sister and to create a fellowship which worships and serves together and which prays for and carries out a mission to the community.

Karl Barth criticizes the family organization as pre-Christian and too tribal and kin-related to be a paradigm for the church.[3] He is correct in making us aware of the possibility of idolatry and over-rootedness in the family. However, Jesus' statement in Mark 3:32-35 points beyond blood kinship to the brother-sister-fellowship feeling within the Kingdom. This appears to me to be ascribing the possibility of an extended family milieu within the church. Yet even the church can become idolatrous and must be challenged to open its doors to the outsider and to extend its mission to the family-less.

2. *Family Enrichment*

For pastors and family-life committees facing the task of enriching family life, the big question is, How should we go about it? Families are fractured and cut off from one another—whether in large cities, suburbs, or rural areas. In cities people who live in the same block keep their distance, one family finding it difficult to relate to another family. Nuclear family living becomes a protective shield against the impersonality experienced. In suburbs different work, school, and recreation schedules take family members to different places at different times, with even dinner no longer bringing people together. In rural areas with shopping areas, consolidated schools, and church located lengthy distances from the home, family members must rely on tight scheduling and transportation and no longer have the time together they once had. Family enrichment may appear to the modern family as just one more program—even the straw that breaks the camel's back. Convincing busy and overburdened church members that their families are fractured shouldn't be difficult. Creating family atmospheres and load-lightening support structures within the church will take planning and work. However, if it can strengthen family life and lift some of the burden of modern living, it will prove worth the effort.

There are three dimensions to strengthening family life which a church may cultivate: (1) a caring dimension; (2) an educational dimension; and (3) an enriching/counseling dimension. I want to describe and illustrate all three aspects, but I shall spend the most time with the last since it has not yet been illustrated sufficiently in writing.

(1) The church should develop a network of caring and express its family concerns through visiting the sick, the grief-stricken, and those who are housebound. Intercessory prayer for those undergoing crisis may become a regular part of the church's order of service. In addition, the minister may mention the names of those about whom the congregation should be concerned and seek volunteers to call upon those persons. Celebrations—births, weddings, anniversaries—are also marked and persons are asked to express the joy of the church family to the participants. The telephone is an instrument of caring for those who cannot travel in person to express the congregation's concern. Note that the congregation is the primary agent of pastoral care with its pastors serving as enablers and consultants as well as visitors.

(2) The church should develop a family ministry through its educational program. This ministry may be effected through intergenerational classes (in the summer when

other classes are slack); intergenerational retreats for the entire church membership, including single, widowed, and divorced persons; and intentional communities where church members live together, buy their food cooperatively, and are involved in missional activity. (The Sojourners Community and the Community of Christ, Washington, D.C., are two examples of the latter.) All these are ways in which groups may study together and develop the family support bonds which such inclusive study generates.

Let me highlight one such example—the Family Clustering model developed by Margaret Sawin and her associates of Rochester, New York. "A family cluster is a group of four or five complete family units who contract to meet together periodically over an extended period of time in order to share learning (educational experiences related to the questions, problems, concerns of their everyday family lives)."[4] They provide mutual support for each other, gain practice in skills which improve the family's living together, and celebrate their beliefs and life together. There are usually twenty to twenty-five persons in a cluster. With the range of ages across the life span, each person has the opportunity to teach another, and each family has the chance to develop what amounts to an intergenerational bond with both older and younger families. Single persons and those separated from their families are included as they used to be in extended families.

A family cluster attempts to help families look at how their family system is operating and behaving, what family members want to do about it and how family members may want to change/grow/be educated. The family cluster helps families intentionalize their way of changing and then provides a secure group in which some new intentionalized behavior can be tried out. The family being present as a complete family unit assures that the new behavior has been exposed to all members and therefore can be utilized in the "back home situation."[5]

This program has some likeness to neighborhood groups which have been developed in some churches with widely dispersed memberships and can be offered as a supplement to the traditional Sunday church school approach to Christian education.

(3) The church should focus finally on family enrichment and counseling. Most family members can be helped to cope with the developmental passage points and accidental crisis periods through enrichment experiences. For this reason the pastor and family life committee should devote the majority of their time to developing enrichment opportunities for families. These should include short-term enrichment experiences for premarital couples, for parents of young children, for parents of adolescents, and for couples in the mid-years—some of whom are involved with "not quite adult" children and who have responsibility for aging parents.[6] Widow to Widow programs, Parents Without Partners groups, assertiveness training for newly liberated women and men; grief recovery groups for those suffering various losses—these and other counseling groups should be organized for family members in crisis times.

Family counseling should be available to those families for whom group interaction and support are not enough to help them through a critical period. The pastor will need to be aware of those who are under stress in the congregation and who draw more attention to themselves and who require more counseling help than an enrichment group can provide (see earlier chapters for assessment and treatment procedures). Social workers, family counselors, and psychiatrists may be members of enrichment groups so that the pastor again need not be anxious about this screening role. He may consult with these family helpers and develop some coordinated group and individual family counseling treament plan which will be of greatest usefulness to the troubled family.

I want now to develop in some detail the Family Enrichment Weekend as illustrative of how a church may go about working with families in an intensive intergenerational weekend. The purpose of the Family Retreat would be spelled out as follows: to enrich family living by bettering communication between family members, by working through current levels of family conflict, by increasing coping skills and management of family problems, and by providing family members with models of intergenerational living. Such a weekend would only be open to families who bring at least one child or one grandparent, since otherwise the intergenerational dimension for family learning would be missing. The minimum number for such a retreat would be three families—which could include eighteen or more people if all had four children or brought grandparents. If there is adequate leadership and available living space, the weekend could include as many as fifty families. I would judge that one family leader is needed for every ten families. If infants and preschool children attend, some child care and craft activity should be arranged so that parents can participate in the small group activity.

Vignette: Family Enrichment Retreat

The theme of the retreat was "Communicating the Christian Faith Across Generations," and we had the participants read the November 1978 edition of *Christian Home* magazine, which was on Christian traditions. Sixteen families from one suburban church went to a church camp which was winterized and in which families could room together. My wife and I were the leaders; and one of our daughters, an elementary school teacher, and a teen-aged neighbor girl who had had experience in a preschool were in charge of children from toddlers to age twelve. The teen-agers participated with their parents and with the grandparents and widowed or divorced parents who were a part of the retreat.

Let me outline and report in an abbreviated way the manner in which the retreat unfolded. We arrived about seven o'clock Friday evening and found our quarters. The first activity, after a light supper, was a get-acquainted session with families making name tags and gathering around a fireside for singing and refreshments. Because of the young children and the intensity of the retreat, everyone went to bed early the first evening.

Saturday morning the small children were taken to their classroom, and the youth and adults gathered in a large room by the fire to work together on the theme of the retreat. I led the first session, "How We Communicate in Families," dealing with the blocks to communication and how families can work through these blocks. We engaged in some communication exercises as families to experience what the particular barriers were and how families resolve these. At the second session, my wife, Alma, discussed how we tell the family story and helped put people in touch with their family narrative. She also took some time to make the group aware of good children's literature which can be used in reading together and in family discussion.

Saturday afternoon the group spent in family recreation: playing volleyball together, going on a hayride, taking walks through the fall woods, horseback riding, and boating on the lake. Families with the smallest children were able to spend time with one another in some kind of activity.

Saturday evening we began by working out our family trees. Each family had been asked to bring pictures of their immediate family, which they pasted on the tree. Families were divided into groups of three and given time to explain their family tree. Then the family trees were put up on the walls of the room and left there to be observed and talked about for the rest of the retreat. Following this period, the older persons went to the top of a hill for a bonfire, hymn singing, and outdoor communion service. The final part of the evening was spent in an intergenerational music listening period with refreshments. We were supposed to talk about music from our generations, but the participants were so exhausted by then that they were content to sit, listen, or play ping-pong.

Sunday I led the group in considering how we learn faith differently at different ages and stages, utilizing the work of Erikson, Kohlberg, and Fowler. As an exercise each family was given time to talk about Christmas traditions, which ones they thought important to keep, and which ones needed rethinking. An hour was free in which families could walk in the woods, talk together, and gather leaves and outdoor materials for a worship center. This, by the way, was placed on a mantle above the fireplace and added greatly to the beauty of the room. I led the final worship and helped the group share what they had learned from their families and what they hoped to pass on to their families about the faith. The beautiful "Sabbath Song" from *Fiddler on the Roof* was learned and sung by the group as a closing theme.

3. *Training Family Aides*

Most pastors soon discover that the need is so great in the family field that they cannot meet it by themselves, nor should they. If the laity have a ministry it surely should be expressed in the family area. However, many laity feel inadequately informed and poorly equipped to aid the pastor in educating, enriching, or counseling families. Therefore, the training task becomes primary for the church leader. If the minister is trained as a family life specialist he can perform the training task. If he is not, the minister can, as stage-manager/director, discover the specialists in the congregation or in the community to direct the training for the church.[7] Family aides, once trained, can increase the supportive and healing work of family ministry tenfold. They can provide the structure of the family life program in education, enrichment and counseling which makes the church a family of families and propels its members into mission to broken and disorganized families in the community.

Family Aide Training Module

The minister or church staff person responsible for family life should be aware of couples both interested in and capable of working with family clusters. These couples can be recruited for training after participation in some family enrichment weekend or series of enrichment experiences. Their motivation is high at that time, and their understanding of providing the experience for other families is keen.[8] The training can be organized as a summer laboratory or take place on several weekends when family clusters or family enrichment groups are meeting. The training module should include:

(1) Observation of a trained family aide working with a family cluster; accompanying a pastor or family aide on a family visit; or viewing a family counseling session through a one-way screen.

(2) Planning one's own leadership of a family cluster; discussing the family background of the family one intends to visit with the pastor or family visitor or developing a counseling approach with a supervisor of the family one intends to talk with.

(3) Participating as a leader of a family cluster—perhaps with one's spouse or another member of one's family as co-leader; making the family visit; conducting the family interview. The interview may be conducted with the supervisor present or behind a

one-way screen or with him observing the interview
on videotape afterward.

(4) Evaluation of the educational, calling, or counseling
process to understand how one functions as a family
aide. This is the most important part of the learning
experience and needs to be carried out with a trained
family life educator and/or family therapist.

A consultant can be employed for designing and
carrying out the training experience if the church has
sufficient funds for such employment. If not, the smaller
church can consider training its pastor or a capable
layperson who may then develop this training module or
the equipping of family aides.[9]

Conclusion

The family is not an outmoded institution, but it should
be apparent by now that its forms and functions are
changing. It is still the best place to raise children, to teach
them values, and to provide comfort and support for men
and women at the various critical stages and emergencies
of their lives. The nuclear family is the form—evolved
within this century—which has proved inadequate to men
and women, boys and girls, to give the emotional supplies
and support they need and to connect them with a
responsible neighborhood. Some alternative to the extended family is necessary today in Western society. The
ways in which this alternative is being wrought out in a
diverse, highly mobile, highly technical society has been
the thrust of this book.

Some families have become so cut off from one another,
so mangled by the stress and impersonal forces of modern
living that they need counseling and therapeutic help. The
minister and church should be willing and able to help
those families who need such help. Ways of understand-

ing and helping such families have occupied more than half of our time. However, the church should also be interested in the growth and development of healthy families across their total life. We have been interested in how families can help themselves go through the nodal events and crisis events. The church is a family of families; and, despite its heresies, its structural rigidities, and its allowing itself to be pushed into the backwaters by fast-moving currents of change, at its best it has brought families into touch with the depths of their existence and enabled family relationships to blossom and grow.

Finally, we have said that leaders in the church—clergy and laity alike—may find their time best spent in training and prevention, in health-producing and family-enriching experiences, rather than in simply doing first-aid and therapeutic work after marriages and families break down. Jesus, our mentor, did say he came to save sinners and not the righteous for the Kingdom. This is represented by the counseling and crisis intervention type of work one does as a minister within a church. He also equipped the seventy for their mission to the Gentiles, and spent all his ministry with the twelve who were to become the bulwark of the church (the family of families). In this spirit we can meet the challenge of today's disintegrating communities and enable today's families to become faithful and on mission to those communities.

Appendix

MARRIAGE AND FAMILY COUNSELING

NAME OF STUDENT_____ INITIALS OF COUPLE
OR FAMILY_____
DATE OF INTERVIEW

_____

A. *Setting*

Describe the couple physically. Report the nonverbal cues (gestures, facial expression, clothing) which you notice when you first meet them. Report presenting problem from both persons. What were the goals of the session? Was a contract established for counseling?

B. *Verbatim*

Report as far as you can the actual dialogue between you and the couple or family. Allow a three-inch space to the right of the dialogue for the instructor's comments. If the session is tape-recorded, select only a portion of the tape for reproduction. Transcribe that portion which for you is most revelatory of the pastoral exchange between you and the couple or family. Report pauses and other nonverbal behavior as one would do in a play dialogue.

C. *Analysis*

The purpose of the analysis is to reflect upon the interview and to understand the dynamics of the helping relationship, as well as the nature of the counseling problem. You should include the following:

1. A dynamic psychological analysis of the couple/family and of yourself. This includes a development of the dynamics of their interrelationship and the relationship between you and the individuals/couple/family; ways you aided and hindered the marriage counseling process; the pastoral issues which emerge specifically from this situation; how well you accomplished or did not accomplish the goals you stated that you wanted to achieve; what discrepancy, if any, do you now see between your intention and your actual performance; and what have you learned personally and pastorally from studying this report about the individuals/couple/family, about yourself, or about your own attitude in relation to the couple/family?

2. A dynamic theological analysis of the whole situation including your part in the process. More specifically, what theological principle, doctrine, issue, or question seems to be supported, challenged, or illuminated? How does your own understanding of the doctrine, issue, or question shed light on the actual situation? As you evaluate the strengths and weaknesses of the couple/family, how does your theological reflection make specific contributions? What are the theological dynamics of this couple/family in their own milieu and in their relationship with you as a potential helper? Be as specific as you can to articulate how your theology helps you to help the couple/family and what pastoral implications have emerged for you as a result of this contact in particular?

3. A critical analysis of your readings is essential and should be integrated into your analysis. More specifically, it is important for you to indicate which writers—theological and secular—and their contributions have directly influenced you, both positively and negatively.

Family History[1]

I.   History of the immediate problem including sequence of events and dates. Look for the main source of anxiety of the precipitant(s) and what or who is feeding it.

II.   Three-generation genogram with important dates, locations, names, moves, occupations, out of contact, level of functioning.

III. History of the nuclear family and description of it, with sequence of nodal events from the time the parents met (e.g., what attracted them to each other?)

A. Nodal events
   1. meeting
   2. courtship
   3. marriage—where, who, etc.
   4. period prior to birth of first child
   5. birth of first child
   6. job changes—locations
   7. children to school
   8. wife to work, etc.

B. Life course of husband was
   1. planned————by default
   2. goal-oriented————by default
   3. few problems————many problems
   4. decisions based on principle vs. decisions based on relationships
   5. individual responsibility vs. dependence on others

      6. carried out in isolation vs. in contact with important relations

      7. productive vs. nonproductive

C. Life course of the wife was
    1. planned———by default
    2. goal-oriented———by default
    3. few problems———many problems
    4. decisions based on principle vs. decisions based on relationships
    5. individual responsibility vs. dependence on others
    6. carried out in isolation vs. in contact with important relations
    7. productive vs. nonproductive

D. Brief description of husband's family and how it functioned (social level; general functioning in response to stress—social, physical, emotional; point out strong people and weak; chronic vs. acute cut-offs; explosive vs. cohesive vs. drifting cut-offs; major triangles and chronic triangles; is it an extincting family or holding its own; low level vs. average vs. unusually differentiated; resourceful vs. collapsing)

E. Brief description of wife's family and how it functioned (social level; general functioning in response to stress—social, physical, emotional; point out strong people and weak; chronic vs. acute cut-offs; explosive vs. cohesive vs. drifting cut-offs; major triangles and chronic triangles; is it an extincting family or holding its own; low level vs. average vs. unusually differentiated; resourceful vs. collapsing)

F. List of the most intensive relationships of the husband and wife according to the degree of intensity:

1. Husband's ball of wax and its fluidity:

Relationship	Quality	Location	Level of Contact
Spouse Children Parents Siblings Friends Other			

2. Wife's ball of wax and its fluidity:

Relationship	Quality	Location	Level of Contact
Spouse Children Parents Siblings Friends Other			

G. Sibling structure of nuclear family
   1. compatible as to sex; compatible as to rank
   2. influence of triangling process

H. Overall differentiation level (functional not basic) of husband, wife, and children over ten years of age; degree of fusion of husband and wife functional togetherness vs. symptomatic togetherness

I. Nuclear mechanisms
  1. distancing
     a. intrapsychic
     b. physical
  2. adaptive spouse
     a. physical
     b. emotional
     c. behavorial
  3. conflict (describe frequency; intensity; and trigger issues)
  4. projection to a child including intensity and degree of triangling and type of symptoms
  5. cut-offs: operational, solid, or permanent?
  6. drift to extended family and degree of dependency
  7. repeat patterns over the generations, e.g.:
     a. conflict of husband and wife
     b. conflict of father and mother
  8. importance of social ties
  9. patriarchy vs. matriarchy
  10. differentiation or lack thereof of the female line

J. Current or recent changes (within two years), stress or crises, e.g.:
  1. revolution
  2. death
  3. illness
  4. children to college
  5. wife to work
  6. marriages
  7. births
  8. divorce
  9. financial crises
  10. job loss

L. Interview:

1. appearance
2. level of anxiety
3. other-oriented vs. definition of problem
4. serious vs. light vs. glib
5. therapist's objectivity

M. Summary of formulation

N. Plans:
   1. immediate plan
      a. decrease the anxiety
      b. define immediate problem
   2. long-term plan
      a. decrease anxiety and worry
      b. research the nature of the problem
      c. focus on husband and wife
      d. focus on extended family
      e. adult one-to-one relationship with each family member: nonconfronting—low key—avoid anxiety pockets
   3. Therapist defines his role for the family and redefines the problem and teaches his viewpoint
      a. Has the therapist been triangled much?
      b. Has the therapist remained outside?
      c. Has he taken sides or overreacted emotionally?
      d. Has he been too distant?
   4. prediction of results
   5. family goals as to change: What is changeable? What is not?

Notes

Preface

[1]Reference will be made to other parts of the globe, but this book has to do with families in the Western world. It should be noted that change is going on in all cultures in the developing nations.

Chapter I

[1]Census Bureau Report, "The Census is in, Marriage is Out" in the *Washington Post*, December 1976, p. C1.

[2]*Ibid.*

[3]*Ibid.*, p. C2.

[4]Susan Byrne, "Nobody Home, The Erosion of the American Family," A conversation with Urie Bronfenbrenner, *Psychology Today*, May 1977, pp. 41 ff.

[5]Margaret Mead and Ken Heyman, *The Family* (New York: Macmillan, 1965), pp. 77, 78.

[6]Reuben Hill, *Modern Systems Theory and the Family: A Confrontation*, in *Sourcebook*, Marvin Sussman, ed. (Boston: Houghton Mifflin, 1974), p. 307.

[7]Byrne, "Nobody Home," p. 45.

[8]Because of the inadequacy of the English language I am forced to use masculine pronouns when speaking generally of a family member. I have attempted to avoid sexist language and to recognize the equal status of women in the family at all places in the discussion.

Chapter II

[1]Mead and Heyman, *The Family*, p. 80.

[2]L. Kluckhohn and H. Murray, *Personality in Nature, Society and Culture* (New York: Alfred A. Knopf, 1953), p. 19.

[3]Philip J. Guerin, Jr., ed., *Family Therapy: Theory and Practice* (New York: Gardner Press, 1976), p. 452.

[4]Paul Wilkes, *Six American Families* (New York: Seabury, 1977). Also,

189

Elliot Wright, *Six American Families* (Viewers Guide, 1525 McGavock St., Nashville, Tenn. 37203, 1977).

⁵Kluckhohn and Murray, *Personality in Nature*, p. 46.

⁶Michael Harrington, *The Other America* (Baltimore: Penguin Books, 1965); and Oscar Lewis, *Children of Sanchez and La Vida* (New York: Random House, 1966).

⁷Robert Lifton, *Death in Life* (New York: Random House, 1967), and other writings.

Chapter III

¹*New York Times*, November 27, 1977, p. 1.

²Mary Jo Bane, *Here to Stay: American Families in the Twentieth Century* (New York: Basic Books, 1976), p. XIV.

³Don Jackson and William Lederer, *The Mirages of Marriage* (New York: Norton, 1968), pp. 87-97.

⁴*Ibid.*, p. 17.

⁵Charles W. Stewart, *The Minister as Marriage Counselor*, rev. ed. (Nashville: Abingdon, 1970), p. 35.

⁶Virginia M. Satir, *Conjoint Family Therapy* (Palo Alto, California: Science and Behavior Books, 1964).

⁷Clifford J. Sager, *Marriage Contracts and Couple Therapy* (New York: Brunner/Mazel Publishers, 1976), p. 26.

⁸See Sager's instrument for working out the marital contract in his Appendix.

⁹*Marriage Contracts and Couple Therapy*, p. 28.

¹⁰*Ibid.*, p. 21.

¹¹See Evelyn). Duvall, *Family Development* (Philadelphia: J. B. Lippincott, 1971), p. 151.

¹²Sidney Jourard, "Marriage is for Life," *Journal of Marriage and Family Counseling*, vol. 1, no. 3, p. 199.

¹³*Ibid.*, p. 203.

¹⁴Daniel Levinson, "Growing up with the Dream," *Psychology Today*, January 1978, p. 31. See also Levinson's *The Seasons of a Man's Life* (New York: Knopf, 1978).

¹⁵Levinson, "Growing Up," p. 31.

¹⁶*Ibid.*

¹⁷Gail Sheehy, *Passages* (New York: Dutton, 1976), pp. 217-35.

¹⁸See Feldman and Ragoff, "Correlates of Change in Marital Satisfaction with the Birth of the First Child," APA Report, September 3, 1968, San Francisco.

¹⁹Paul Graubard, *Positive Parenthood* (New York: Bobbs Merrill, 1977).

²⁰See description in my book *Adolescent Religion* (Nashville: Abingdon, 1967), pp. 13-25.

²¹J. E. Marcia, "Development and Validation of Ego Identity Status," *Journal of Personality and Social Psychology* 3 (1966), pp. 551-59.

²²Sheehy, *Passages*, p. 15.

Chapter IV

[1]Gerald Caplan, *Principles of Preventative Psychiatry* (New York: Basic Books, 1964).

[2]David Lynn, *The Father: His Role in Child Development* (Monterey, California: Brooks/Cole, 1974), p. 90.

[3]Caplan, *Principles of Preventative Psychiatry*, p. 40.

[4]Virginia M. Satir, *People Making* (Palo Alto, California: Science and Behavior Books, 1972), p. 113.

[5]See chapter 10 for discussion of these possible programs.

[6]Caplan, *Principles of Preventative Psychiatry*.

[7]Lois B. Murphy and Alice Moriarity, *Vulnerability, Coping and Growth* (New Haven: Yale University Press, 1976), p. 332. See also, Charles W. Stewart, *Adolescent Religion*, pp. 32-57.

[8]W. Robert Beavers, "The Application of Family Systems Theory," in David K. Switzer, *The Minister as Crisis Counselor* (Nashville: Abingdon, 1974), pp. 184-85.

[9]Erik Erikson, *Identity and the Life Cycle* (New York: International University Press, 1959), p. 61.

[10]Gordon Allport, *Religion in the Developing Personality* (New York: Academy of Religion and Mental Health, University Press, 1960), p. 33.

[11]"Machismo & Marianismo" in *Society*, Sept./Oct. 1973, quoted in *Readings in Human Sexuality: Contemporary Perspectives, 1976-77*. Chad Gordon and Gaye Johnson, eds. (New York: Harper & Row, 1976), pp. 71-96.

[12]Lynn, *The Father*, p. 85.

[13]See Jay Haley, *Problem Solving Therapy* (San Francisco: Jossey Bass, 1978), for excellent discussions both of family rules and family hierarchy.

[14]See Murray Bowen, "Theory in the Practice of Psychotherapy" in *Family Therapy*, Philip Guerin, ed., pp. 65-66 for discussion of fusion, triangles, and the emotional cutoff.

Chapter V

[1]*motive* magazine, November 1965, p. 5.

[2]David Mace, *The Christian Response to the Sexual Revolution* (Nashville: Abingdon, 1970), pp. 40 ff.

[3]See Charles W. Stewart, "How Effective Are Our Marriage Ministries?" in *Pastoral Psychology*, Summer 1977, p. 260.

[4]Richard Wilkes, *The Pastor and Group Marriage Counseling* (Nashville: Abingdon, 1974), p. 18.

[5]"How Effective Are Our Marriage Ministries?" pp. 266-67.

[6]*Ibid.*, p. 263.

[7]William H. Masters and Virginia E. Johnson, *Human Sexual Inadequacy* (Boston: Little, Brown, 1970).

[8]See my *Minister as Marriage Counselor*, where I develop Paul Tillich's principle of correlation with respect to marriage.

[9]Daniel Day Williams, *The Minister and the Care of Souls* (New York: Harper, 1961), p. 61.

[10]John B. Cobb, Jr., *Theology and Pastoral Care* (Philadelphia: Fortress Press, 1977), p. 3.

Chapter VI

[1]*Problem Solving Therapy*, p. 105.

[2]See Philip Guerin for a history of the family therapy movement as well as an excellent compendium of the present leaders in the family therapy movement. *Family Therapy: Theory and Practice.*

[3]Charles W. Stewart, *The Minister as Marriage Counselor*, rev. ed. (Nashville: Abingdon, 1970), p. 39.

[4]Referral is dealt with at the end of the chapter.

[5]*Why* questions get at motives of which most family members are uncertain, allow them to rationalize, to transcend the family dilemma, and to refuse responsibility for problem solving.

[6]Virginia Satir, *Conjoint Family Therapy*, pp. 106-59.

[7]P. Guerin and E. Pendagast, cf. chap. 2, n. 3 *Family Therapy*, p. 457.

[8]Paul Steinhauer and Rae-Grant, *Psychological Problems of the Child and His Family* (Toronto: Macmillan of Canada, 1977), pp. 83-84. See also, J. Rich, *Interviewing Children and Adolescents* (New York: Macmillan, 1968), and D. W. Winnicott, *Therapeutic Consultations in Child Psychiatry* (Basic Books, 1971).

[9]See Karl Menninger, Marty Mayman, and Paul Pruyser, *A Manual for Psychiatric Case Study* (New York: Grune and Stratton, 1962).

[10]A note on note taking: A counselor keeps a fact sheet and shorthand or abbreviated notes in a file or notebook on each family counseling session. Even though a pastor has a good memory, once he begins to see four or five families at a time, he will begin to get the details of each family's interrelationships mixed up and soon may find himself unable to sort out these details in the counseling session. Notes which he can review before each session will help him avoid this confusion and also help him in thinking through the problem with the family.

[11]See J. Luft, *Of Human Interaction* (Palo Alto, California: Mayfield Publishing Co., 1969), reported in S. Eisenberg and D. Delaney, *The Counseling Process* (Chicago: Rand McNally, 1977), p. 78.

[12]See Haley, *Problem Solving Therapy*, pp. 48-80, for an excellent discussion on giving directives.

[13]M. Bowen, "Theory in the Practice of Psychotherapy" in *Family Therapy*, p. 86.

Chapter VII

[1]"Personal Reflections of the Family Therapist," in *Journal of Marriage and Family Counseling,* January 1975, p. 25.

[2]Mary Jo Bane, *Here to Stay,* p. 37.

[3]U. Bronfenbrenner, "American Families: Trends and Pressures" (Washington: U.S. Government Printing Office), pp. 138-48.

[4]Names and places have been changed in the case to protect the identity of the family.

[5]Carl Whitaker, "Four Dimension Relationship" in Philip Guerin, *Family Therapy,* p. 184.

Chapter VIII

[1]Study on Family (National Academy of Sciences).

[2]David B. Lynn, *The Father: His Role in Child Development,* p. 266.

[3]Mary Jo Bane, *Here to Stay,* p. 12.

[4]Murray Bowen, "Family Reaction to Death" in Philip Guerin, ed., *Family Therapy, Theory and Practice,* p. 339.

[5]E. Mavis Hetherington, "Girls Without Fathers," in *Psychology Today,* February 1973, p. 49.

[6]Muriel Fisher, "Dealing with Death in the Family," *New York Times* magazine, March 13, 1977, p. 86.

[7]Eda LeShan, *Learning to Say Goodbye* (New York: Macmillan, 1976), pp. 17-41.

[8]Richard Hunt, in David Switzer, *The Minister as Crisis Counselor,* (Nashville: Abingdon Press, 1974), pp. 235-36.

[9]J. Louise Despert, *Children of Divorce* (New York: Dolphin, 1962), pp. 32-33.

[10]Salvadore Minuchin, *Families and Family Therapy* (Cambridge: Harvard University Press, 1974), p. 98.

Chapter IX

[1]Minuchin, *Families and Family Therapy,* p. 50.

[2]See Charles W. Stewart, *Adolescent Religion* for studies of early adolescent value struggles.

[3]Daniel Yankelovich, reported in the *New York Times.*

[4]Robert Sorensen, *Adolescent Sexuality in Contemporary America* (New York: World Publication Co., 1973), pp. 59-60.

[5]Merton Strommen, *The Five Cries of Youth* (New York: Harper, 1974), p. 97.

[6]Erich Berne, *Games People Play* (New York: Grove Press, 1964).

[7]David Lynn, *The Father: His Role in Child Development,* p. 248.

[8]Murray Bowen, Triangles (Georgetown University, 1974 workshop), p. 35.

[9]Peggy Papp, "Family Choreography" in Philip Guerin, ed., *Family Therapy*, pp. 465-79.

[10]Virginia Satir, *Conjoint Family Therapy*, p. 60.

[11]Lynn Hoffman, "Breaking the Homeostatic Cycle" in Philip Guerin, *Family Therapy*, p. 504.

[12]David Lynn, *The Father*, p. 282.

[13]Jay Haley, *Problem Solving Therapy*, p. 53.

[14]Derek Miller, *Adolescence: Psychology, Psychopathology and Psychotherapy* (New York: Jason Aronson, 1974) is a good basic text to help the pastor understand adolescent delinquency.

Chapter X

[1]Helen Caplan, *Helping the Helpers to Help* (Greenwich, Connecticut: Seabury Press, 1972), p. 35.

[2]John Wilkenson, "Christian Healing and the Congregation" in *The Healing Church* (Geneva: World Council of Churches, 1965), p. 31.

[3]Karl Barth, *Church Dogmatics*, vol. 3, part 4 (Edinburgh: T. & T. Clark, 1961), p. 241.

[4]Margaret Sawin, "The Theoretical Assumptions of the Family Cluster Model" Unpublished paper, 1977.

[5]*Ibid*. Family Clustering is one of several such plans which have been worked out in this decade. One should write to Family Clustering, P.O. Box 8452, Rochester, NY 14618, for more information. Consultants who will train leadership for family clusters and hold Family Clustering Conferences are available for churches and other groups interested in working out the program.

[6]See Howard J. Clinebell, *The People Dynamic* (New York: Harper, 1972) for discussion of family enrichment opportunities for each of these age groups.

[7]Pastors in isolated or poorly staffed areas may inquire at the county welfare department, state health institution, or a branch of the state university for names of such persons.

[8]See my article, "Training Church Laymen as Community Health Workers" in *Community Mental Health, Role of Church and Temple*, H. J. Clinebell, ed., Nashville: Abingdon, 1970, pp. 194-200.

[9]See National Council of Churches, one's denominational department of marriage and family life, or independent training organizations located in many parts of the country concerned with equipping laity for education and counseling.

Appendix

[1]Adapted from A. Delano Hagin.

Selected Bibliography

I. Psychological and Theological Backgrounds

Bane, Mary Jo. *Here to Stay: American Families in the Twentieth Century*. New York: Basic Books, 1976.

Barth, Karl. *On Marriage*. Philadelphia: Fortress Press, 1968.

Bernard, Jessie. *The Future of Marriage*. New York: World Publishing Co., 1972.

Clinebell, Howard and Charlotte. *The Intimate Marriage*. New York: Harper & Row, 1970.

Cole, William. *Sex and Love in the Bible*. New York: Association Press, 1959.

Duvall, Evelyn, and Hill, Reuben. *Being Married*. New York: Association Press, 1960.

Haughton, Rosemary. *The Theology of Marriage*. Notre Dame, Indiana: Fides Publishers, 1971.

Hunt, Morton. *Sexual Behavior in the 1970's*. New York: Playboy Press, 1974.

Kerns, Joseph. *The Theology of Marriage: Historical Development*. New York: Sheed & Ward, 1964.

Komarovsky, Mirra. *Blue Collar Marriage*. New York: Random House, 1964.

Lederer, William, and Jackson, Don. *The Mirages of Marriage*. New York: W. W. Norton, 1968.

Levinson, Daniel. *The Seasons of a Man's Life*. New York: Alfred A. Knopf, 1978.

Lynn, David B. *The Father: His Role in Child Development*. Monterey, California: Brooks Cole, 1974.

McCary, James. *Freedom and Growth in Marriage*. Santa Barbara, California: Hamilton Publishing Company, 1975.

195

Mace, David. *The Christian Response to the Sexual Revolution.* Nashville: Abingdon, 1970.

Masters, William, and Johnson, Virginia. *The Pleasure Bond.* Boston: Little Brown, 1975.

Money, John, and Tucker, Patricia. *Sexual Signatures: On Being a Man or a Woman.* Boston: Little Brown, 1975.

O'Neill, Nena and George. *Open Marriage: A New Life Style.* New York: Evans, 1972.

Pittenger, Norman. *Making Sexuality Human.* Philadelphia: Pilgrim Press, 1970.

Presbyterian Church USA General Assembly Commission on Marriage, Divorce and Remarriage. *Sexuality and the Human Community.* Philadelphia, 1970.

―――. *Towards A Quaker View of Sex.* London: Friends House, 1964.

Rogers, Carl. *Becoming Partners: Marriage and its Alternatives.* New York: Delacorte Press, 1972.

Sheehy, Gail. *Passages: Predictable Crises of Adult Life.* New York: Dutton, 1976.

Sherfey, Mary Jane. *The Nature and Evolution of Female Sexuality.* New York: Random House, 1972.

Sussman, Marvin, ed. *Source Book in Marriage and the Family,* 4th ed. Boston: Houghton Mifflin, 1974.

Thielicke, Helmut. *The Ethics of Sex.* New York: Harper & Row, 1964.

Von Allman, Jean. *Pauline Teaching on Marriage.* London: Faith Press, 1963.

II. Marriage Counseling

Bertalanffy, L. V. *General System Theory.* Harmondsworth, England: Penguin, 1973.

Dicks, H. V. *Marital Tensions.* London: Routledge & Kegan Paul, 1967.

Egleson, James and Janet. *Parents Without Partners.* New York: Dutton, 1961.

Emerson, James. *Divorce, the Church and Remarriage.* Philadelphia: Westminster Press, 1961.

Epstein, Joseph. *Divorced in America.* New York: Penguin, 1975.

Fitzgerald, R. V. *Conjoint Marital Therapy.* New York: J. Aronson Publishing Co., 1973.

Green, Bernard, ed. *The Psychotherapies of Marital Disharmony.* New York: Free Press, 1965.

Group for the Advancement of Psychotherapy (GAP). *Assessment of Sexual Function.* Vol. 8, No. 8 (1973).

Gurman, A. S., and Rice, A. G. *Couples in Conflict.* New York: J. Aronson, 1975.

Hardy, Richard. *Creative Divorce Through Social & Psychological Approaches.* Springfield, Illinois: Thomas, 1974.

Kaplan, Helen S. *The New Sex Therapy.* New York: Brunner/Mazel, 1974.

Krantzler, Mel. *Creative Divorce.* New York: M. Evans, 1973, 1974; distributed by Lippincott, Philadelphia.

Martin, Peter. *A Marital Therapy Manual.* New York: Brunner/Mazel, 1976.

Masters, William, and Johnson, Virginia. *Human Sexual Inadequacy.* Boston: Little Brown, 1970.

Nash, Ethel; Jessner, Lucy; and Abse, D. W. *Marriage Counseling in Medical Practice.* Chapel Hill: University of North Carolina Press, 1964.

Porter, Sylvia. *The Money Book.* Garden City, N.Y.: Doubleday, 1975.

Sager, Clifford. *Marriage Contracts and Couple Therapy.* New York: Brunner/Mazel, 1976.

Satir, Virginia. *People Making.* Palo Alto: Science & Behavior Books, 1972.

Steinzer, Bernard. *When Parents Divorce.* New York: Pantheon, 1969.

Stewart, Charles W. *The Minister as Marriage Counselor.* Nashville: Abingdon, 1970.

Switzer, David. *The Minister as Crisis Counselor.* Nashville: Abingdon, 1974.

Taves, Isabella. *Women Alone.* New York: Funk & Wagnalls, 1968.

III. Family Counseling

Ackerman, Nathan. *The Psychodynamics of Family Life.* New York: Basic Books, 1958.

Bowen, Murray. *Family Therapy in Clinical Practice: Collected Papers of Murray Bowen.* New York: Aronson, 1978.

Chance, Erika. *Families in Treatment.* New York: Basic Books, 1959.

Erikson, Erik. *Childhood and Society*. New York: W. W. Norton, 1950.

————. *Identity, Youth and Crisis*. New York: W. W. Norton, 1968.

Freud, Anna. *The Ego and the Mechanisms of Defense*. New York: International Universities Press.

Gordon, Sol. *The Sexual Adolescent*. N. Scituate, Mass.: Duxbury Press, 1973.

Group for the Advancement of Psychotherapy (GAP). *Treatment of Families in Conflict*. New York: Aronson, 1970.

Guerin, Philip. *Family Therapy, Theory and Practice*. New York: Gardner Press, 1976.

Haley, Jay. *Problem Solving Therapy*. San Francisco: Jossey-Bass, 1978.

Josselyn, Irene. *Adolescence*. New York: Harper & Row, 1971.

Miller, Derek. *Adolescence: Psychology, Psychopathology and Psychotherapy*. New York: Aronson, 1974.

Minuchin, Salvadore. *Families and Family Therapy*. Cambridge: Harvard Press, 1974.

Murphy, Lois, and Moriarity, Alice. *Vulnerability, Coping and Growth: From Infancy to Adolescence*. New Haven: Yale University Press, 1976.

Napier, Augustus Y. with Whitaker, Carl A. *The Family Crucible*. New York: Harper & Row, 1978.

Papp, Peggy, ed. *Family Therapy: Full Length Case Studies*. New York: Gardner Press, 1977.

Satir, Virginia. *Conjoint Family Therapy*. Palo Alto: Science and Behavior Books, 1967.

Staples, Robert. *The Black Family*. Belmont, California: Wadsworth Publishing Company, 1978.

Steinhauer, Paul, and Rae-Grant, Quentin. *Psychological Problems of the Child and His Family*. Toronto: Macmillan of Canada, 1977.

Stewart, Charles W. *Adolescent Religion*. Nashville: Abingdon, 1967.

Strommen, Merton. *The Five Cries of Youth*. St. Louis: Concordia, 1974.

Watzlawick, P.; Weakland, J.; and Fisch, R. *Change*. New York: W. W. Norton, 1974.

IV. Group Counseling and Marriage Enrichment

Bach, George, and Wyden, Peter. *The Intimate Enemy*. New York: Morrow, 1969.

Bell, John E. *Family Therapy*. New York: Aronson, 1975.

Burton, Arthur. *Encounter, the Theory and Practice of Dynamic Encounter Groups*. San Francisco: Jossey-Bass, 1969.

Clinebell, Howard. *Growth Groups, Marriage and Family Enrichment*. Nashville: Abingdon, 1977.

Knowles, Joseph. *Group Counseling*. Englewood Cliffs: Prentice-Hall, 1964.

Leslie, Robert. *Sharing Groups in the Church*. Nashville: Abingdon, 1971.

Mace, David R. and Vera. *We Can Have Better Marriages if We Really Want Them*. Nashville: Abingdon, 1974.

Maslow, Abraham. *The Farther Reaches of Human Nature*. New York: Viking, 1971.

Oden, Thomas. *Game Free, A Guide to the Meaning of Intimacy*. New York: Harper & Row, 1974.

————. *The Intensive Group Experience*. Philadelphia: Westminster Press, 1972.

Otto, Herbert. *Marriage and Family Enrichment: New Perspectives and Programs*. Nashville: Abingdon, 1976.

Reid, Claude. *Groups Alive—Church Alive*. New York: Harper & Row, 1969.

Rogers, Carl. *On Encounter Groups*. New York: Harper & Row, 1970.

Schutz, William. *Joy, Expanding Human Awareness*. New York: Grove, 1967.

————. *Here Comes Everybody*. New York: Harper & Row, 1971.

Smith, Leon. *Family Ministry, An Educational Resource for the Local Church*. Nashville: Disciple Resource, 1975.

Wilke, Richard. *The Pastor and Marriage Group Counseling*. Nashville: Abingdon, 1974.

V. Films, Teaching, Audio and Video Tapes

Family Life Literature and Films: An Annotated Bibliography. 1972, 1974. Available from Minnesota Council on Family Relations, 1219 University Avenue, SE, Minneapolis, MN 55414.

Audiotapes from American Association for Marriage and Family Therapy. Write C. Jay Skidmore, 1425 Maple Drive, Logan, UT 84321 for list.

Audiotapes from American Academy of Psychotherapists. Write AAP Tape Library, 1040 Woodcock Road, Orlando, FL 32802.

Videotapes of Murray Bowen (Family Systems Therapy and Psychotherapy). Write The Family Center, Dept. of Psychiatry, Georgetown University School of Medicine, 4380 MacArthur Blvd., NW, Washington, DC 20007.

Videotapes of Salvadore Minuchin and associates. Philadelphia Child Guidance Clinic, No. 2 Children's Center, 34th and Civic Center Blvd., Philadelphia, PA 19104.

Videotapes of Virginia Satir. Write Science and Behavior Books, P.O. Box 11457, Palo Alto, CA 94306.

Videotapes and Interviews with Prominent Family Therapists. Write Frederick Duhl, Boston Family Institute, 1170 Commonwealth Ave., Boston, MA 021334.

Index